The

LITTLE
GREEN
SPOON

The LITTLE GREEN SPOON

Deliciously healthy
home-cooking to
share and enjoy

INDY POWER

EBURY
PRESS

This book is dedicated to my great grandmother, Baba, who I so wish could have seen it come to life. To Tom, my chief taste-tester and kindest critic, to my Mom and Dad for all of their love, inspiration and encouragement and to Sallyanne, for helping to make this dream come true. My little Arnold too, who keeps me company in the kitchen every day.

Most of all, it's for all of you. For anyone who has ever made my recipes or followed The Little Green Spoon, thank you for letting me do what I love and for loving it too.

10 9 8 7 6 5 4 3 2 1

Ebury Press, an imprint of Ebury Publishing,
20 Vauxhall Bridge Road,
London, SW1V 2SA

Ebury Press is part of the Penguin Random House group of companies whose addresses can be found at global.penguinrandomhouse.com

 Penguin
Random House
UK

Text © Indy Power 2016

Indy Power has asserted her right to be identified as the author of this Work in accordance with the Copyright, Designs and Patents Act 1988

First published by Ebury Press in 2016

www.penguin.co.uk

A CIP catalogue record for this book is available from the British Library

Project editor: Louise McKeever
Design: Smith & Gilmour
Photography: Martin Poole
(except for the pages listed below)
Food stylist: Aya Nishimura
(except for the pages listed below)
Prop stylist: Liz Belton
(except for the pages listed below)

Photographs on pages 24, 30, 57, 62, 78, 84, 91, 94, 110, 116, 122, 130, 138, 148, 154, 160, 170, 176 and 224 courtesy of Indy Power

ISBN: 978 1785032 769

Colour origination by Rhapsody Ltd London
Printed and bound in China by Toppan Leefung

Penguin Random House is committed to a sustainable future for our business, our readers and our planet. This book is made from Forest Stewardship Council® certified paper.

 MIX
Paper from
responsible sources
FSC® C018179

CONTENTS

INTRODUCTION

I started my blog, The Little Green Spoon, in October 2013 thanks to encouragement from my hungry family, and began sharing my healthy recipe experiments. I am so honoured that my little blog has allowed me to to make my dream of writing a cookbook come true and I hope that you love making and eating these recipes as much as I do.

I believe eating healthily all comes down to taste. Everyone would eat well if healthy meals tasted like their favourite foods. I want to show that they can. My way of eating isn't about deprivation or giving things up, it's about feeling nourished, happy and satisfied and enjoying every bite.

When I was little my mother gave me everything the adults ate, from curries and teriyaki to veggie bakes and roasts. She didn't adapt recipes to suit children or make bland baby foods – we all ate exactly the same food, no matter how spicy or complex the flavours were. Years later, our favourite family pastime is talking about food, cooking and eating together. To me, food is far, far more than just fuel. It's one of the nicest things about being alive and the benefits of eating well extend to every part of life.

In school, I was all about cupcakes. I baked almost every day as a counterpoint to study. Then one day it dawned on me that I couldn't go on stuffing myself and everyone around me with sugar and flour forever. I stripped back to the healthier basics and straight away everything started tasting better and I started feeling amazing. At the time, there was no science or method behind how I did it, but I took note of everything and realised that once I gave up refined sugar and gluten, cut back on dairy and upped my protein intake (I always ate tons and tons of veg),

I was like a new person. My eating transformation took a while – I gave things up gradually. I didn't go cold turkey because I wasn't under any pressure to change, I was just experimenting and liking what was happening.

For me, the biggest improvement I experienced was with my mood. It's no secret that gut bacteria affects our digestion and metabolism, but there is growing research into how much it can influence our brains. Foods such as gluten and sugar can irritate the gut, which may cause a range of problems such as digestive issues, allergies, anxiety and depression. Going by my own body and mind, as well as what I've learned from studying Nutrition and Health Coaching, I truly believe gut health to have a huge influence on mental wellness and find that eating right helps me to take control of my mind, keeping anxiety and depression at bay. For me it's happy gut, happy mind!

I also noticed huge changes in my digestion and skin and the better I felt, the more I valued good nutrition. I had started out life as a meticulous label-reader because I'm allergic to peanuts. As a nervous little kid I used to fret over the contents of every bite, but as I reached my late teens I started to embrace all other nuts as well as a more carefree attitude towards food in general. It was really liberating to relax a little and enjoy all of the amazing food I could have, rather than focusing on what I couldn't.

Now I've come full circle and am back to rigorous label reading, but this time by choice! I like to know exactly what goes into what I eat and pick what's best for me. At the same time, I don't obsess about every sub-atomic particle that enters my body like some diet evangelists do. I feel it's healthier, mentally at least, to do the best you can. Make healthy food that's incredibly delicious and your best gets a lot better.

I also believe that if you crave something sweet, you shouldn't deprive yourself, but rather indulge in gorgeous natural foods. Conjure a chocolate bar or a mince pie out of purer ingredients and you can still enjoy treats. Likewise, sometimes the only thing for it after a big night out or a hard work week is serious comfort food, so I reimagine healthier versions of classic savoury dishes. Pasta becomes courgetti (page 11), bread goes grain free (page 112) and chickpea flour replaces batter on fish (page 92). I've discovered loads of tricks and workarounds to get where my body likes to be, without compromising my taste buds and natural greed.

I also take a lot of inspiration from my travels, adapting discoveries like tortillas (page 108) and miso broccoli (page 51). Japanese flavours permeate quite a few of my recipes too as my grandmother is Japanese and many of my earliest food memories surround sushi and New Year's banquet tables groaning with delicacies.

Cost is really important to me – less is certainly more since I've only just finished college. Good food is an investment in your health, so it's definitely worth spending a little extra when you can, but it should also be accessible for everyone. Simplicity is also key because I like to be able to whip things up depending on my spontaneous cravings and you can't always have hours to spend in the kitchen.

I'm only at the beginning of what I hope will be a lifelong learning curve about balancing taste, nutrition and creativity to make exciting, satisfying meals for everyone I love (even Arnold, my itchy French bulldog) and these are a collection of my favourites so far. Eating, cooking and being healthy are my favourite things and despite what some people think, they are not mutually exclusive. Food is pleasure, it's emotive, and eating food that tastes incredible and nourishes your body makes you feel great. I'd take a raw home-made caramel square full of nuts and healthy fats over a bag of crisps any day. I want to make people fall in love with healthy food, the way it tastes, the way it looks and the way it makes them feel. Just as I have.

This book is bursting with delectable recipes that I cook every day, whether it's a last-minute lunch, a gorgeous dinner feast or a decadent dessert. I get my inspiration from whatever I'm in the mood for, my travels, whatever's in season and, sometimes, just whatever's in my tiny fridge! I hope this book will help people on their own personal journey to eating and feeling better. The younger you start, the better – but it's never too late. My dad has just figured out he can use chickpea flour in the bread he's made every week forever (Daddy Bread, page 112) and everyone who tastes it raves about it even more than they used to. Any dog can learn new tricks.

My recipes are to be shared with those around you; they're for everyone, whether you've got allergies, intolerances or digestive issues, or you're just trying to cut down on processed foods or sugar and nourish your body with real food. This book isn't about cutting things out, it's about embracing all of nature's gorgeous natural foods to make you feel amazing. And it's not as hard as it sounds. Everything you need is in here and I've guided you through each recipe with Dairy-Free, Gluten-Free, Vegan and Paleo symbols, so you can make sure you're eating what you decide is best for you, while enjoying every mouthful.

HOW TO...

Here are a few simple tips on how to cook and prepare some of the ingredients used in this book that you may be less familiar with. Use this section as a guide to techniques alongside the recipes.

How to Cook Quinoa

Quinoa is so delicious, but it is underrated and even disliked by many people because it is often cooked badly. When it's not cooked right it can be too soggy, too dry, bitter or flavourless. Unless you've had it cooked correctly, don't write it off just yet. Cooked well, quinoa is fluffy and light and compliments most savoury dishes, as well as being amazing at absorbing other flavours.

Here is the foolproof way to make perfect quinoa every time (or almost every time, I admit I have forgotten about it and burnt it more than once!). The most important and absolutely crucial tip is that you must use stock rather than water. You can use white, red or black quinoa, but personally white is my favourite. Hot or cold, it goes with everything.

The recipe here works for all kinds of quinoa and makes about four servings (double or triple as needed, but make sure to use the same ratio of quinoa to stock).

MAKES 3–4 SERVINGS

500 ml (17 fl oz/2 cups) chicken or vegetable stock

170 g (6 oz/1 cup) quinoa

Add the cold stock to a pot on a medium heat. Use a medium-sized pot – you don't want it to be too big. Add the uncooked quinoa in on top and stir so that all of the quinoa is submerged.

Pop the lid on the pot and leave the quinoa to bubble away for about 13–15 minutes, then check it. The quinoa is almost ready when you can see only a little liquid and air pockets forming. When all of the visible liquid has been absorbed (the quinoa should still be a little soggy, but there should be barely any separate liquid remaining), take the pot off the heat and fluff the quinoa with a fork.

Pop the lid back on for another 5 minutes, still off the heat, to allow it to steam and any remaining moisture to be absorbed. Remove the lid and fluff once more before serving.

How to Cook Buckwheat

You can cook buckwheat in a very similar way to quinoa, just with a little less stock. Again, it can take some trial and error to figure out when exactly to take it off the heat, but practice makes perfect.

MAKES 4 SERVINGS

180 g (6 oz/1 cup) buckwheat groats

435 ml (14 fl oz/1¾ cups) chicken or vegetable stock

Add the cold stock to a pot on a medium heat. Add the buckwheat groats and stir so that all of the buckwheat is submerged.

Pop the lid on the pot and leave the buckwheat to bubble away for about 12 minutes until all of the visible liquid has been absorbed. Watch the buckwheat carefully for the last few minutes as you don't want to overcook it. As soon as there is no visible liquid left, take it off the heat and fluff the buckwheat with a fork.

Pop the lid back on, still off the heat, and let it steam for a few more minutes. Remove the lid and fluff again before serving.

How to Spiralize Courgettes

If you have a hand-held spiralizer, chop off one end of the courgette and place it in the spiralizer. Then, exactly like sharpening a pencil, twist the courgette, pushing as you twist, until beautiful courgette ribbons form. You can stop twisting every few turns and then start again so the ribbons aren't too long. If you're using a countertop spiralizer, insert your desired blade. Chop the end off the courgette and press one end onto the spikes near the blade and the other end on the spikes attached to the handle, then simply twist and push and watch the ribbons come out the other end!

How to Make Oat Flour

Oat flour is great for baking as it works in a really similar way to white flour. Although you can find it in some supermarkets, I've never found gluten-free oat flour so I always make my own and keep it in a jar in the cupboard. It's really simple – all you need is a blender and some gluten-free oats. If you have a high-powered blender or food processor you'll be able to get it really fine, really quick. Otherwise, just blend until it's as fine as you can get it.

MAKES 120 G (4¼ OZ/1½ CUPS)

120 g (4¼ oz/1½ cups) gluten-free oats

Add the gluten-free oats to your blender and blend on high until you have a very fine flour.

Scrape down the edges and repeat once more to make sure the oats are evenly ground.

Use straight away or store in an airtight container or jar.

How to Make Nut Milk

My personal favourites are almond and cashew milk, but you can use any kind of nut to make nut milk and it's so simple. Just don't forget to soak your nuts the night before!

MAKES 1 LITRE (1¾ PINTS/4 CUPS)

300 g (10 oz/2 cups) nuts

you will need: a nut milk bag/cheesecloth

Soak your nuts in the fridge overnight.

Drain and rinse the nuts and then add them to your blender with 1 litre (1¾ pints/ 4 cups) of fresh water.

Blitz on high for about 30 seconds until the nuts are completely broken down. Then repeat once more.

Hold your nut milk bag over a big jug or bowl. Pour the mixture slowly through the nut milk bag into the jug, squeezing as you go, until all of the liquid has run through. Discard all of the mushy nuts or use them for something else. What's left in your bowl/jug is your delicious nut milk!

Store in your fridge for 3 days in a covered jug or sealed bottle. A little separation is natural, just shake before serving.

How to Poach an Egg

The eternal mystery! Good poached eggs taste amazing but for some reason, poaching an egg perfectly is inordinately difficult and there are so many different methods for doing it. Thankfully, I recently learned the amazingly easy and foolproof way to perfect poachies – thank you Steve and James at Daylesford Cookery School!

MAKES 1 POACHED EGG

1 egg

1 teaspoon apple cider or red wine vinegar

pinch of coarse salt

Fill a medium saucepan with water and bring it to a boil. This is crucial, you want a proper boil, not just a simmer. When it is boiling, submerge your egg (still in its shell) under the water for 12 seconds. Then take it out and set it aside. Add the vinegar and salt to the water.

Turn down the temperature until the water is simmering. Crack your egg and hold it just above water level, as close as you can get without burning your fingers, before opening it carefully to let the egg slide gently into the water.

Run a spoon swiftly through the water once around the sides of the saucepan, this will help to shape the egg.

Turn off the heat and pop the lid on. Set a timer for 4 minutes. When the timer goes off, use a large spoon to remove the egg from the water and plate your perfectly runny poachy.

How to Make Nut Butter

Everybody loves nut butter! It's the best snack or treat and it's really easy to make if you have a little patience. You can make nut butter out of all kinds of nuts: pistachios, pecans, hazelnuts, cashews – they're all amazing and they all have their own unique flavour. You can also experiment with different flavourings, such as adding ground cinnamon or cacao powder and maple syrup. In this book there are a few special flavours, but the basic recipe for any nut butter is below. The key is to roast the nuts before; this gives them more flavour and releases their oils, which speeds up the blending process.

300 g (10 oz/2 cups) of your desired nuts

Roast the nuts (see right).

When they're done, add the warm nuts to your food processor (along with any spices or flavourings) and blend on high, scraping down the sides as needed. The amount of time it takes to turn to butter will depend on how powerful your food processor is – it can take anywhere from a few minutes up to 20 minutes. However long it takes, don't lose faith, just keep blending!

The nuts will break down into a flour, clump together into a ball and then liquefy into a gorgeous butter. The longer you blend, the runnier it will be.

How to Toast Nuts and Seeds

Toasting nuts and seeds absolutely transforms them. I sprinkle nuts and seeds on almost everything, but never without toasting them. For seeds, I always toast them in a pan. For nuts, you can either roast them or toast them in a pan. Roasting tends to give a much more even result and it's easier not to burn them, but toasting them in a pan is great if you're short on time.

If using a pan, add the nuts/seeds to the pan on a medium/high heat and toast them, tossing frequently, until golden and fragrant. You don't need to add oil – they will release plenty. Seeds will start to pop and look plump when they're ready.

For roasting nuts, follow the oven temperatures and approximate time instructions below, depending on the type of nut. For all nuts, toss halfway through cooking and keep an eye on them. The times below are an estimate and how fast your nuts roast will depend on your oven.

Almonds: 180°C for 12–14 minutes

Cashews: 180°C for 8 minutes

Hazelnuts: 180°C for 12–15 minutes

Pecans, pistachios and walnuts: 180°C for 8–10 minutes

GOOD
MORNINGS

EVERYTHING GRANOLA

GF **DF** **V**

MAKES 8-10 SERVINGS

150 g (5 oz/1½ cups)
gluten-free oats

45 g (1½ oz/½ cup)
desiccated coconut

110 g (4 oz/¾ cup)
whole nuts (almonds,
cashews, pistachios, etc
or a combination)

75 g (2½ oz/½ cup) dried
fruit (cherries, apricots,
raisins, etc or a
combination)

2 tablespoons seeds
(chia, pumpkin, sunflower,
etc or a combination)

25 g (¾ oz/½ cup)
coconut chips

75 g (2½ oz/½ cup)
coconut sugar

125 ml (4 fl oz/½ cup)
coconut oil

This granola is so crispy and crunchy and you can add in anything and everything you like. Use up any miscellaneous nuts or seeds you have lying around and adjust this recipe to your taste to create delicious granola just the way you like it.

Preheat the oven to 170°C/325°F/Gas mark 3.

Combine the oats, desiccated coconut, nuts, dried fruit, seeds and coconut chips in a large bowl.

In a saucepan, melt the coconut sugar and coconut oil together on a medium heat until all the coconut sugar is melted and you have a glossy mixture. Don't worry if the coconut sugar and oil separate.

Pour the melted mixture into the dry ingredients gradually, while mixing, until well combined.

Spread the mixture out on a baking sheet lined with parchment paper and bake for about 25 minutes until golden brown and crispy. Toss twice throughout the cooking time.

Store in an airtight jar for up to 1 month.

RASPBERRY BUCKWHEAT PANCAKES

SERVES 3

125 g (4 oz/1 cup) buckwheat flour

2 eggs

2 tablespoons maple syrup/honey

2 tablespoons melted coconut oil

1 teaspoon vanilla essence

1 teaspoon baking powder

250 ml (8½ fl oz/1 cup) almond milk, unsweetened

100 g (3½ oz/¾ cup) raspberries

coconut oil, for frying

These pancakes will make you so happy. Buckwheat flour creates light-as-air pancakes and they're so easy to whisk up. Adding fruit or berries elevates them to a new level and raspberries have an amazing colour and tartness. Make these pancakes for brunch, piled high in a big stack in the centre of the table for sharing with a scoop of coconut cream and a drizzle of maple syrup.

Add everything except for the almond milk and raspberries to your food processor and blitz until well combined.

Gradually add in the almond milk and blend until you have a smooth, quite thick, but still runny mixture. If the mixture is too thick, add in another dash of almond milk.

Add the mixture to a jug and stir in the raspberries. Heat some coconut oil in a pan on a medium heat. Drizzle in enough mixture for your desired pancake size.

Cook until little bubbles form in the centre and then flip. Cook for another 30 seconds on this side until golden brown and then plate. Continue with the other pancakes, adding more coconut oil as necessary, stacking them on top of each other to keep them warm.

BANANA PECAN BAKED OATS

SERVES 2-4

1 banana

1 egg

2 tablespoons maple syrup

25 g (1 oz/¼ cup) pecans

100 g (3½ oz/1 cup) gluten-free oats

250 ml (8½ fl oz/1 cup) almond milk

½ teaspoon ground cinnamon

This is the most comforting way to start the day, whether you're snuggled up for a winter breakfast in bed or sitting outside on a sunny morning. Banana and oats are a lovely combination and pairing them with toasted pecans, cinnamon and a hint of maple syrup is just sublime. It does takes a little time to cook, but your taste buds will thank you for your patience. It will fill your kitchen with the most wonderful smell, too.

Preheat the oven to 180°C/350°F/Gas mark 4.

Halve the banana and add one half to a large bowl. Add in the egg and maple syrup and whisk until you have a wet, mushy mixture.

Roughly chop the pecans and add them to the bowl along with the oats, almond milk and cinnamon.

Pour the mixture into your baking dish. Slice the other half of the banana and arrange the slices on top.

Bake for about 30 minutes until the centre is set but not completely dry and the top is golden brown. Serve hot.

JUST PEACHY BIRCHER MUESLI

SERVES 4

100 g (3½ oz/1 cup) gluten-free oats

45 g (1½ oz/½ cup) desiccated coconut

50 g (2 oz/½ cup) flaked almonds

1 heaped tablespoon chia seeds

2 peaches

375 ml (13 fl oz/1½ cups) almond milk, unsweetened

2 tablespoons maple syrup/honey

A great breakfast that you can make ahead of time, yet tastes just as fresh and delicious as something made on the spot. The textures of the oats, coconut and flaked almonds taste heavenly soaked in the beautiful peaches and creamy almond milk. It will keep for 3–5 days in an airtight container in the fridge, so make it in a big jar and keep it for a few mornings. After the first day, top it up with a bit more almond milk to revitalize it a little before serving.

Add the oats, coconut, flaked almonds and chia seeds to a large bowl and mix them all together.

Remove the stones from the peaches and add the flesh to your food processor with the almond milk and sweetener. Pulse until smooth.

Add the peach mixture to the dry ingredients and mix well. Cover the bowl, or add it into a large jar, and pop it in the fridge overnight (or for a minimum of 3 hours).

Serve as is or with a dash more almond milk and whatever toppings you like.

SMOKED SALMON, PEAS AND DILL WITH POACHED EGGS

SERVES 2

200 g (7 oz) frozen peas

1 handful of fresh dill

150 g (5 oz) smoked salmon

2 eggs

1 tablespoon olive oil

1 lemon

coarse salt and pepper

Smoked salmon and eggs together are a dream, in every sense. They make a perfectly balanced breakfast, full of protein and healthy fats, and they won't leave you feeling bloated and full. This is a great way to spruce up the classic pairing and it only takes a few extra minutes. Dill, smoked salmon and lemon are made for each other, then add in some peas and a runny poached egg and you've got the ultimate breakfast.

Start by boiling your peas for about 3 minutes. Don't forget about them or they'll overcook.

While the peas are on, remove any thick stalks from the dill sprigs and finely chop the leaves. Then, chop the smoked salmon into small chunks.

Drain the peas and rinse them with cold water to stop the cooking process. Put your eggs on to poach (page 12).

Add the peas, dill and salmon to a large bowl and drizzle in the olive oil and the juice of half the lemon. Sprinkle with coarse salt and toss everything together.

Divide the pea mixture between two plates.

When the eggs are cooked to your liking, pop one on top of each plate.

Chop the remaining half lemon into wedges and serve alongside with a sprinkling of pepper.

GRAIN-FREE MAPLE PECAN GRANOLA

GF DF V P

SERVES 8

100 g (3½ oz/1 cup) pecans, roughly chopped

120 g (4 oz/1 cup) ground almonds

50 g (2 oz/½ cup) desiccated coconut

100 g (3½ oz/1 cup) flaked almonds

100 g (3½ oz/1 cup) pumpkin seeds

1½ teaspoons ground cinnamon

60 ml (2 fl oz/¼ cup) melted coconut oil

60 ml (2 fl oz/¼ cup) maple syrup

Granola can be one of the yummiest treats for breakfasts and such a moreish snack. This one is completely grain free but full of crispy, crunchy clusters and flavourful toasted nuts. The maple syrup makes everything extra crisp and coats the toasted pecans, making them even more delicious. This is for those mornings when only something sweet will do – sprinkle it over tart coconut yoghurt with a mountain of berries for the ultimate breakfast satisfaction. Keep a jar at the back of the pantry for when your sweet tooth comes knocking.

Preheat the oven to 180°C/350°F/Gas mark 4.

Add the pecans to a large bowl with the ground almonds, desiccated coconut, flaked almonds, pumpkin seeds and cinnamon and mix well.

Drizzle in the melted coconut oil and maple syrup and mix well to combine.

Spread the mixture out in a thin layer on a baking sheet lined with parchment paper and bake for 20–25 minutes until golden and crisp. Toss twice during the cooking time so that the granola crisps evenly.

Leave it to cool completely before breaking the granola up into clusters. Store in an airtight jar or container for up to 1 month.

CACAO OVERNIGHT OATS

SERVES 1

50 g (2 oz/½ cup)
gluten-free oats

1 heaped teaspoon
cacao powder

up to 125 ml (4 fl oz/
½ cup) almond milk

1 tablespoon maple
syrup/honey

Overnight oats are the best busy bee breakfast when you're
in a hurry. They only take a few minutes to prepare the night
before and you can just grab them at the last minute. Cacao
powder (see page 213) is an amazing source of antioxidants,
fibre, magnesium, calcium and iron so you can enjoy this
chocolatey and luxurious breakfast knowing you've had
a fantastic start to the day. This tastes like such a treat it
also doubles as a delicious dessert.

In a bowl, combine the oats and cacao powder. Then add
them to your jar.

Pour in as much of the almond milk as you need, depending
on how thick you like your oats.

Stir in a tablespoon of sweetener and mix well.

Seal your jar and pop in the fridge overnight (or for a
minimum of 3 hours) before enjoying.

BUCKWHEAT WAFFLES
WITH MAPLE PECANS

GF **DF**

SERVES 2

125 g (4 oz/1 cup)
buckwheat flour

2 eggs

2 tablespoons maple
syrup/honey

2 tablespoons melted
coconut oil

1 teaspoon vanilla essence

1 teaspoon baking powder

pinch of coarse salt

1 banana

250 ml (8½ fl oz/1 cup)
almond milk, unsweetened

For the pecans:

25 g (1 oz/¼ cup) pecans

1 tablespoon maple syrup

This might just be the best breakfast in the whole world. The waffles are light and fluffy with a lovely sweetness and the maple-toasted pecans have an amazing crunch – each bite tastes more indulgent than the last. If you don't have a waffle iron, you can easily make these as pancakes using the exact same recipe. I serve mine with a scoop of coconut cream, berries and a drizzle of maple syrup.

Preheat your oven to 180°C/350°F/Gas mark 4.

First prepare the pecans. Mix the pecans and maple syrup together in a bowl so that all of the nuts are coated. Spread them out on a baking sheet and bake for about 8 minutes, until crisp.

Add all of the waffle ingredients except for the banana and almond milk to your food processor and blitz until well combined.

Add in the banana and a dash of the almond milk and blend. Gradually add in the rest of the almond milk. You should have a smooth, quite thick but still runny mixture. If the mixture is too thick, add in another dash of almond milk.

Pour a ladle of the mixture into the centre of your waffle iron and cook for 7–8 minutes, depending on your machine. Repeat with the remaining mixture.

Serve the waffles hot with the maple pecans sprinkled on top.

PINA COLADA CHIA PUDDING

SERVES 1

250 ml (8½ fl oz/1 cup) coconut milk

50 g (2 oz) fresh pineapple

3 tablespoons chia seeds

TO TOP: desiccated coconut, coconut chips, more pineapple, etc

This is one breakfast certain to put a pep in your step. Every tropical bite tastes like a mini holiday – it'll put you in such a good mood! Chia seeds are such amazing little seeds, full of fibre and protein and packed with omega-3 fatty acids, and chia pudding is a great way to get them into your diet. It's so luxurious and creamy that it also makes a delicious dessert.

Add the coconut milk and pineapple to your blender and blitz until smooth.

Add the chia seeds to a jar and pour in the pineapple milk. Stir well and leave it to sit for about a minute. Then stir again, letting it sit for about 5 minutes this time. Stir one last time and pop in the fridge overnight or for a minimum of 3 hours.

Serve topped with desiccated coconut, coconut chips or more fresh pineapple chunks.

BLUEBERRY BUCKWHEAT PORRIDGE

SERVES 2

180 g (6 oz/1 cup)
buckwheat groats

250 ml (8½ fl oz/
1 cup) water

500 ml (17 fl oz/2 cups)
almond milk

2 tablespoons maple
syrup/honey

For the blueberry sauce:

125 g (4 oz/1 cup)
blueberries

2 tablespoons water

OPTIONAL: strawberries,
coconut, nuts, seeds,
nut butter

This is a recipe from my blog, which I just couldn't leave out. I've always loved porridge, but buckwheat porridge is extra special – it tastes like a creamy rice pudding. I crave it and have it for dessert as often as for breakfast. It looks particularly pretty, too.

Add the buckwheat and water to a saucepan on a medium heat. Let it cook until almost all of the water is absorbed, then add in half of the almond milk and again, cook until almost all of the liquid is absorbed.

Next, add in the sweetener and the rest of the almond milk. Cook until the buckwheat is soft and the porridge is your desired runniness.

While the porridge is cooking, make the blueberry sauce. Add the blueberries and water to a saucepan on a medium heat. When the water is hot, use a potato masher or fork to squish the blueberries. Keep squishing and stirring for about 3 minutes until you have a gorgeous deep purple/ blue sauce.

Pour the porridge into your bowls and spoon in the blueberry sauce. Top with any additional toppings and serve.

DIPPY EGGS AND SWEET POTATO SOLDIERS

SERVES 1

1 large sweet potato

1 tablespoon olive oil

2 eggs

coarse salt and pepper

My dad used to always make us dippy eggs, with endless batches of salt and peppery soldiers, and it's still everybody's favourite breakfast in my house. This is my version, with crispy sweet potato soldiers instead of toast to soak up the runny yolks. Hopefully you approve, Dad!

Preheat the oven to 200°C/400°F/Gas mark 6.

Peel your sweet potato and slice it into soldiers/fries. Drizzle them with olive oil and sprinkle generously with salt and pepper. Use your hands to toss them around, making sure they're all evenly coated in oil, salt and pepper.

Cook for 30–35 minutes until crispy on the outside and soft on the inside. Taste them to see if they're done!

A few minutes before they're done, boil your eggs. When the water is boiling, add the eggs and cook them for exactly 4½ minutes for perfectly dippy eggs.

Place the eggs in egg cups, using a spoon to crack the tops open, with the soldiers surrounding them. Sprinkle everything with salt and pepper before serving.

FIG AND CINNAMON
QUINOA PORRIDGE

SERVES 2

85 g (3 oz/½ cup) quinoa

125 ml (4 fl oz/
½ cup) water

250 ml (8½ fl oz/1 cup)
almond milk, unsweetened

3 ripe figs

½ teaspoon vanilla
essence

½ teaspoon ground
cinnamon, plus extra
to sprinkle

1 tablespoon maple
syrup/honey

Pictured overleaf

Quinoa porridge is perfect for when you want a filling and hearty breakfast but don't want to skip out on the protein. At the end of summer, this is the best way to ease yourself into colder autumn mornings and make the most of all the amazing fresh figs around at that time of year. The combination of sticky figs and cosy cinnamon is hard to beat, so make this while you can – the fig season is lamentably short. If it's the wrong time of year, sub in some mashed banana instead.

Add the quinoa, water and half of the nut milk to a medium-sized saucepan on a medium heat. Pop the lid on and let it cook for about 13 minutes until most of the liquid has been absorbed and it's nice and fluffy.

Cut two of the figs in half and scoop the fruity flesh from the inside, then add it to a bowl. Use a fork to mash it up, then stir it into the quinoa with the vanilla, cinnamon and remaining nut milk. Cut the last fig into slices.

Let the quinoa simmer for another few minutes until it has reached your desired consistency, then stir in the sweetener.

Pour the porridge into your bowls, top with the fig slices and sprinkle on a little more cinnamon before serving.

MASALA OMELETTE

GF **DF** **P**

SERVES 1

2 eggs

2 spring onions

1 handful of fresh coriander, plus extra to garnish

3–4 cherry tomatoes

½ teaspoon garam masala

¼ teaspoon ground turmeric

¼ teaspoon paprika

½ teaspoon coconut oil

coarse salt

This is no ordinary omelette, but it's just as easy! If you have eggs for breakfast most days, it's always worth trying out new ways to change them up. Whenever you fancy a break from the norm, these spices will wake up your palate. The recipe's so little effort that you'll be whipping up these omelettes all the time.

Add the eggs to a bowl and whisk.

Finely chop the spring onions, coriander leaves and tomatoes, add them to the eggs with the spices, whisking well.

Add the coconut oil to a small frying pan on a medium heat. When it's melted and hot, pour in the egg mixture and swirl it so it spreads out evenly across the pan.

Cook for about 2 minutes on each side and either fold the omelette over or keep it flat.

Serve with a sprinkle of salt and some fresh coriander.

GRILLED SALMON BENEDICT

SERVES 2

2 salmon fillets, skinless

1 tablespoon olive oil

1 portion of Healthy Hollandaise (page 123)

4 eggs

1 avocado

coarse salt

Eggs Benedict is usually reserved for fancy brunches out, but you can make this at home no problem and it's sure to impress. Grilled salmon makes a nice change from the regular smoked salmon and eggs pairing you usually find. This dish delivers, but won't leave you feeling stodgy and full. Promise.

Lay your salmon fillets out on a roasting tray lined with foil. Drizzle over the olive oil and sprinkle with coarse salt.

Pop them under the grill at 250°C (485°F) for about 12 minutes. They are ready when they flake easily.

While the salmon is cooking, make your hollandaise and then poach your eggs (page 12).

Cut your avocado in half and remove the pit and skin. Cut it into slices and lay them out on your plates. Lay the salmon on top, then add your poached eggs. Drizzle over the hollandaise generously and serve.

CARROT AND COURGETTE FRITTERS WITH POACHED EGGS

GF **DF**

SERVES 4

2 medium carrots, peeled and grated

2 medium courgettes, grated

35 g (1½ oz/¼ cup) pine nuts

2 eggs, whisked

65 g (2½ oz/½ cup) chickpea/gram flour

coconut oil, for frying

1–2 eggs per person

coarse salt and pepper

This breakfast is perfect for long weekend mornings when you have a little extra time. It doesn't get much better than a runny yolk dripping between these crispy fritters. Everybody loves them and they're so versatile – they also make a great starter if you're having people over. Serve them with lots of dips, like my Raita (page 128) or Beetroot Hummus with Roasted Pistachios and Coriander (page 133). You can even use them as a creative substitute for burger buns.

Add the grated carrot and courgette to a large bowl.

Toast the pine nuts in a dry pan on a medium heat until they're golden brown and fragrant.

Add the pine nuts, whisked eggs and chickpea gram flour into the bowl with a good pinch of coarse salt and pepper. Use your hands to mix everything together.

Add about a tablespoon of coconut oil to a pan on medium/high heat. When it's melted and sizzling, use your hands to form a golf-ball-sized ball of the batter (it won't stick together perfectly) and then press it into the pan, flattening it.

Repeat until your pan is full and let the fritters cook for 3–4 minutes on each side until brown and really crispy.

While they're sizzling away, poach your eggs (page 12).

Repeat until all of the batter is finished, adding more coconut oil as necessary.

Divide the fritters among your plates and top each with a poached egg (or two!)

SMASHED EGGS WITH OLIVE OIL AND PROSCIUTTO

SERVES 1

2 eggs

2 slices of prosciutto

1 handful of rocket

1 tablespoon olive oil

coarse salt and pepper

This protein-packed breakfast works wonders as a snack, too. Smashed eggs are so delicious. Cooked just right, so they're still a little gooey but also nice and crumbly, they soak up the olive oil perfectly and dazzle when paired with prosciutto and rocket. Drizzle the olive oil on generously with a good pinch of salt and pepper and you'll be licking the plate.

Add your eggs to boiling water and boil them for about 7 minutes. You want them somewhere between dippy and hard.

While they're cooking, plate your prosciutto and rocket.

After the eggs have boiled for 7 minutes, drain the hot water and cover them with fresh cold water, leaving them to cool for a minute or two. Then, one by one, place them in a small glass or cup and, using your hand to cover the top, shake vigorously to crush the shell. Remove the egg from the glass and peel it with ease. Repeat with the other egg.

Smash the eggs on the plate using a knife and fork.

Drizzle everything with the olive oil and give it a good sprinkle of salt and pepper.

SOUPS, SIDES AND SALADS

SPICED CORN SOUP WITH SESAME AND CHIVES

SERVES 4

1 tablespoon coconut oil

1 teaspoon ground cumin

1 teaspoon paprika

1 teaspoon ground ginger

1 white onion, diced

1 garlic clove, minced

2 medium carrots

320 g (11 oz) sweetcorn

750 ml (1⅓ pints/3 cups) chicken or vegetable stock

80 ml (2½ fl oz/⅓ cup) coconut milk

2 tablespoons sesame seeds

4 chives, finely chopped

coarse salt and pepper

This soup is sweet and perfectly spiced with cumin, paprika and ground ginger for extra kick. You can whip this up in a few minutes and it will taste like you spent hours over the hot stove. It's tough for a soup to be versatile, but this one certainly is – it makes an exquisite lunch or dinner, whatever the weather!

Add a tablespoon of coconut oil to a large pot on a medium heat. Add in the spices and let them heat up in the oil.

Add the the onion and garlic to the pot and toss them so that the onion is evenly coated in the spices. Let the onion soften while you prepare the carrots.

Cut the carrots in half, lengthways, and then chop them into half discs and add them to the pot. Toss everything again, season with a good pinch of coarse salt and then pop the lid on, letting the carrot and onion sweat for about 5 minutes.

Add in the corn and toss. Pop the lid on for another 2–3 minutes.

Add the stock to your food processor with the contents of the pot. Blend until completely smooth.

Pour back into the pot and stir in the coconut milk. Leave to simmer over a medium heat while you make the topping.

Add the sesame seeds to a dry pan on a medium/high heat and sprinkle with coarse salt. Let them cook for a few minutes, stirring occasionally, until they start to pop.

Serve the soup topped with the toasted sesame seeds, chives and coarse salt and pepper to taste.

TOM'S SWEET POTATO SALAD

GF

SERVES 4

4 large sweet potatoes

4 rashers of streaky bacon

3 spring onions

10 cornichon pickles

For the dressing:

60 g (2 oz/¼ cup) Greek yoghurt

2 teaspoons wholegrain mustard

2 tablespoons red wine vinegar

1 tablespoon olive oil

coarse salt and pepper

Potato salad is my boyfriend's all-time favourite dish. I think he'd have it for breakfast, lunch and dinner if he could, so this recipe was a long time coming. When he called it 'the best potato salad' he'd ever had, I knew it was something worth sharing. This recipe is really fresh. It's a welcome contrast to the stodgy potato salad you sometimes see and it's packed full of flavour and texture. There's something incredible about the combination of the vinegary, creamy mustard dressing, the crispy bacon, crunchy cornichons and fresh spring onion and the subtle sweetness of the sweet potatoes. The cornichons are the key, so add in loads!

Place a large pot of water on a high heat to boil. Peel your sweet potatoes. When the water is boiled, add in the sweet potatoes. Boil for 15–20 minutes until tender when pricked with a fork. You want them soft but not mushy.

While the potatoes are boiling, add the bacon to a pan on a medium heat and cook it to your liking. When cooled, chop into little chunks and add it to a large bowl. Slice the spring onions and cornichons into thin discs and add them in too.

Combine all of the dressing ingredients in a bowl and season with salt and pepper to taste.

When the potatoes are done, drain them and leave them to cool completely. When they're cool, slice them into bite-size chunks and add them to the bowl. Pour on the dressing and toss everything well.

KALE MINESTRONE

GF **DF** **V**

SERVES 6

2 tablespoons olive oil

2 garlic cloves, minced

1 white onion, diced

3 celery stalks, chopped

1 carrot, chopped

750 ml (1⅓ pints/3 cups) chicken or vegetable stock

2 x 400 g (14 oz) tins chopped tomatoes

100 g (3½ oz) curly kale, stalks removed and roughly chopped

1 courgette, chopped

1 x 400 g (14 oz) tin cannellini beans, drained

85 g (3 oz/½ cup) quinoa

1 handful of fresh basil, chopped

2 tablespoons balsamic vinegar

coarse salt and pepper

Pictured overleaf

Minestrone is somehow both light and really hearty. This recipe uses quinoa instead of pasta, which absorbs all of the flavours as it cooks, and I've added curly kale, which is just divine after bubbling away in the yummy tomato broth. A little hint of balsamic vinegar makes this minestrone extra special. The key to this recipe is not to rush it – letting it simmer for an hour or more makes such a difference and is well worth the wait. The longer the better.

Heat a large pot on a medium heat and add in the olive oil. Add the garlic to the oil, letting it cook for about 2 minutes.

Add the onion, celery and carrot to the pot and cook for about 5 minutes, stirring regularly.

Add in the stock and tinned tomatoes and stir. Add the kale and courgette to the pot and turn the heat down to low, letting it simmer for about 30 minutes.

After 30 minutes add the beans, quinoa, chopped basil and balsamic vinegar to the pot and let it simmer for another 30 minutes.

Serve with a sprinkling of salt and pepper.

SAGE AND LEMON SWEET POTATO WEDGES

SERVES 4

2 lemons

1 large handful of fresh sage

3 garlic cloves, minced

3 tablespoons olive oil

4 sweet potatoes

coarse salt and pepper

These are no ordinary sweet potato wedges. The sage and lemon zest make a crispy coating that packs in the flavour. They're perfect for every occasion – you really can eat them with anything!

Preheat the oven to 200°C/400°F/Gas mark 6.

Zest the lemons into a bowl. Juice one of them and add the juice to the bowl. Finely chop the sage and add it to the bowl with the garlic, salt and pepper. Drizzle in the olive oil and stir everything around.

Leaving the skin on the sweet potatoes, wash and then chop them into wedges. Add them to a large bowl and pour in the oily sage rub.

Use your hands to toss everything around, making sure all of the wedges are coated well.

Spread the sweet potatoes out in a roasting tray, drizzling and scattering any leftover sage mixture over them. Roast for about 35 minutes or until they reach your desired crispiness.

TENDERSTEM BROCCOLI WITH MISO AND BLACK SESAME

SERVES 2

1 tablespoon black sesame seeds

200 g (7 oz) Tenderstem broccoli

2 tablespoons sweet miso paste

1 tablespoon tahini

2 tablespoons olive oil

juice of ½ lemon

My mom always used to make broccoli with a miso dipping sauce when I was little and whenever I think of broccoli, it comes to mind. This is my version, though I've never actually asked her what's in hers. I use Tenderstem broccoli so you can double dip them into the creamy miso dressing. The toasted black sesame seeds are there for crunch and they look fabulous speckled across the creamy beige dressing.

Bring a large pot of water to the boil.

While the water is heating up, add the black sesame seeds to a dry pan on a medium heat and toast them for a few minutes until they start to pop.

Add the broccoli to the water and boil for 3–4 minutes, just until tender with a little crunch.

While the broccoli is on, combine the miso paste, tahini, olive oil and lemon juice and whisk well.

Plate the broccoli, drizzle over the sauce and sprinkle on the toasted sesame seeds.

WHOLE ROASTED CAULIFLOWER WITH TURMERIC, POMEGRANATE AND TAHINI

GF

SERVES 4-6

1 medium cauliflower

1 teaspoon ground turmeric

1 tablespoon olive oil

2 tablespoons pine nuts

60 g (2 oz/¼ cup) Greek yoghurt

1 tablespoon tahini

juice of 1 lemon

4 tablespoons pomegranate seeds

1 handful of fresh coriander

coarse salt

This is really special. The flavours are incredible together and it looks like a masterpiece in the middle of the table.

Preheat the oven to 180°C/350°F/Gas mark 4.

Cut off the outer leaves of the cauliflower and place it in a roasting tray. Combine the turmeric and olive oil and mix well. Drizzle and rub this all over the cauliflower, then sprinkle on a good pinch of coarse salt.

Roast for 70–80 minutes, until tender on the inside and starting to brown on top.

A few minutes before the cauliflower is done, add the pine nuts to a dry pan on a medium heat and toast them for a few minutes until golden brown.

Combine the Greek yoghurt, tahini and lemon juice and mix together well.

When the cauliflower is done, take it out and place it on your serving plate. Add a big dollop of the sauce to the top of the cauliflower and sprinkle with the toasted pine nuts, pomegranate seeds and a little coriander. Serve with extra sauce on the side.

CURRIED QUINOA AND CHICKPEAS WITH RAITA

SERVES 6

250 g (9 oz/1½ cups) quinoa

750 ml (1⅓ pints/3 cups) chicken or vegetable stock

1 tablespoon curry powder

1 red onion

240 g (8½ oz) chickpeas, soaked or tinned

1 serving of Raita (page 128)

This dish can be served two ways – hot, drizzled with the refreshing raita, or cold, with the raita mixed in for a picnic-style salad. However you have it, let it fill your kitchen and your plate with flavour.

Add the quinoa, stock and curry powder to a pot on a medium heat. Pop the lid on and let it simmer away for about 13 minutes.

While that's cooking, dice the red onion and drain the chickpeas. Add them both to a large bowl.

After about 13 minutes, almost all of the liquid should be absorbed but the quinoa should still be a bit too mushy. Remove the lid and take the pan off the heat. Fluff the quinoa with a fork and then pop the lid on for a few more minutes (still off the heat) allowing the grains to absorb any excess liquid.

Fluff the quinoa again and then add it to the bowl with the chickpeas and onion. Toss everything together.

If serving hot, plate the quinoa with a generous drizzle of raita. If serving cold, mix the raita into the cold quinoa and serve like a pasta salad.

CHICKPEA, AVOCADO
AND FETA SALAD

GF

SERVES 4-6

1 red onion, finely diced

2 ripe avocados, pit
and skin removed and
flesh cubed

50 g (2 oz) feta, cubed

240 g (8½ oz) chickpeas,
soaked or tinned, drained

8–10 cherry tomatoes

1 large handful of fresh
coriander, finely chopped

juice of 2 limes

3 tablespoons olive oil

coarse salt and pepper

This is like a very chunky salsa and is yummy on its own
or piled on top of whatever else you're having. The crisp red
onion, crumbly feta, sweet tomatoes, creamy avocado and
fresh herbs provide the perfect balance of soft and crunch.
There's no cooking involved so you can throw this together
at the last minute.

Add the onion, avocado and feta to a large bowl with the
drained chickpeas.

Quarter the cherry tomatoes and add them to the bowl.
Add the coriander in on top.

Drizzle in the lime juice and olive oil and sprinkle in a good
pinch of salt and pepper. Toss everything well and serve.

ROAST PUMPKIN AND BUTTERNUT SQUASH SOUP

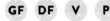

GF **DF** **V** **P**

SERVES 4

700 g (1 lb 9 oz) pumpkin (I use a Golden Nugget pumpkin)

300 g (10½ oz) butternut squash

3 tablespoons olive oil, plus extra for serving

3 garlic cloves

1 teaspoon ground cumin

1 teaspoon ground ginger

1 teaspoon ground turmeric

1 white onion, roughly diced

750 ml (1⅓ pints/3 cups) chicken or vegetable stock

1 handful of pumpkin seeds

coarse salt and pepper

This is hands down my favourite soup ever. It's from my blog and I just couldn't leave it out. It is autumn in a bowl, all those delicious and warming flavours that give us a reason to look forward to that time of year. There's no better dinner to come in out of the cold to and this bowl of comfort will leave you feeling warm and cosy.

Preheat the oven to 200°C/400°F/Gas mark 6.

Scoop out, peel and chop your pumpkin and squash into cubes. This is a bit tedious so if you're short on time, buy it ready prepared.

Lay out the cubes in a roasting tray, drizzle on about a tablespoon of olive oil and sprinkle with a good pinch of coarse salt. Add the three garlic cloves (still in their skins) and toss it all around. Roast for about 30 minutes until soft.

About 25 minutes in, put a large pot on a medium heat and add in 2 tablespoons of the olive oil. Sprinkle in the spices and let them sizzle for a minute.

Add the onion to the pot, letting it sweat for a few minutes and stirring regularly until it is translucent and soft.

Pour in your stock.

Take the roasted pumpkin and squash out of the oven. Squeeze the garlic cloves out of their skins and add them to the pot with the pumpkin and squash. Let it simmer for about 10 minutes.

Add everything to your blender, either in batches or all at once depending on the size of your blender, and blitz until smooth and creamy. Add it all back to the pot and let it simmer while you toast the pumpkin seeds.

Add the seeds to a dry pan on a medium/high heat and toast them for a few minutes until they're nice and plump. Then serve the soup with a sprinkling of seeds, a pinch of salt and pepper and a drizzle of olive oil.

MOROCCAN QUINOA PILAF WITH RAISINS AND PISTACHIOS

SERVES 4

1 tablespoon coconut oil

1 teaspoon ground cumin

½ teaspoon ground cinnamon

1 teaspoon paprika

1 red onion, diced

500 ml (17 fl oz/ 2 cups) stock

170 g (6 oz/1 cup) quinoa

35 g (1¼ oz/¼ cup) golden raisins

35 g (1¼ oz/¼ cup) pistachios

This is my favourite side in the book. While cooking quinoa in stock gives it lots of flavour, there is so much more that can be added to this grain. This combination is just exquisite, with gorgeous sweetness from the cinnamon and raisins, a little heat from the paprika, beautiful fragrance from the cumin and delicious roasted nuttiness and crunch from the pistachios.

Preheat the oven to 180°C/350°F/Gas mark 4.

Add the coconut oil to a large pot on a medium heat. When it's melted, add in the spices and let them sizzle.

Add in the onion and toss everything. Let it cook for about 5 minutes, stirring frequently, until the onion is soft and sweet.

Add in the stock and quinoa and pop the lid on. Let it simmer until all of the visible liquid is gone (about 13 minutes) and then take it off the heat. Stir in the raisins and then pop the lid back on to allow any remaining liquid to be absorbed and the raisins to swell.

Roast the pistachios in the preheated oven for about 8 minutes until fragrant and toasted.

Remove the lid from the quinoa and fluff it with a fork, then add it to your serving bowl, tossing in the roasted pistachios.

TAHINI AND POMEGRANATE COURGETTI SALAD

GF DF V P

SERVES 4

2 large courgettes

25 g (1 oz/¼ cup) flaked almonds

4 tablespoons pomegranate seeds

20 g (¾ oz/1 cup) fresh parsley

For the dressing:

2 tablespoons tahini

3 tablespoons olive oil

juice of 1 lemon

coarse salt and pepper

This is such a beautiful, simple salad. The pomegranates add a stunning pop of colour and tangy sweetness, which works a treat with the rich nuttiness of the tahini. Have it on its own or as a side with some chicken or fish.

Spiralize your courgettes into a large bowl.

Add the flaked almonds to a dry pan on a medium heat and toast them for a few minutes until golden brown.

Combine all of the dressing ingredients in a bowl and whisk them really well until you have a smooth, runny mixture.

Add the pomegranate seeds and toasted almonds to the courgetti (I keep a little of each back for sprinkling on top) and pour on the dressing. Toss everything well and scatter on the remaining almonds and pomegranate.

Roughly chop the parsley and sprinkle on top.

HALLOUMI, AVOCADO
AND LIME SALAD

GF

SERVES 4

100 g (3½ oz) halloumi

100 g (3½ oz) greens
(lamb's lettuce, baby
spinach, etc)

25 g (1 oz) beetroot shoots
or sprouts

2 tablespoons mixed
seeds (sunflower,
pumpkin, sesame, etc)

1 avocado

For the dressing:

juice of 1 lime

1 tablespoon balsamic
vinegar

2 tablespoons olive oil

1 garlic clove, minced

This is a favourite of mine from my blog. This chapter
wouldn't be complete without some halloumi – whenever
it's involved you can count me in, but this in particular is
such a dreamy salad. Creamy avocado, crispy halloumi and
crunchy toasted seeds all drizzled with a lime vinaigrette.
I not only love how this salad tastes, but it looks so bright
and beautiful – a feast for the eyes and the taste buds!

Slice the halloumi into thin strips. Add it to a pan on a
medium/high heat and let it cook for a few minutes on
each side until speckled golden.

While the halloumi is cooking, plate your greens and sprouts.

When the halloumi is done, set it aside and add the seeds
to the pan. Let them cook for a few minutes until toasted
and plump.

Cut your avocado in half and remove the pit and skin. Slice
the avocado flesh and add it to the greens with the halloumi.

Combine all of the dressing ingredients and whisk well.
Drizzle the dressing over everything and sprinkle the salad
with the toasted seeds before serving.

QUINOA RAINBOW SLAW

SERVES 4

85 g (3 oz/½ cup) quinoa

250 ml (8½ fl oz/1 cup) chicken or vegetable stock

1 red pepper, deseeded

¼ red cabbage

1 Baby Gem lettuce

3 spring onions

3 tablespoons mixed seeds (pumpkin, sunflower, sesame, etc)

1 portion of Lemon Vinaigrette (page 129)

This is the perfect accompaniment to almost any meal. Sometimes you just need something that tastes amazing and goes with everything, and this slaw is one of my must-have fridge fillers for a busy week. It's so bright and beautiful and has such a satisfying crunch.

Cook your quinoa in the stock until light and fluffy (page 10), then set it aside to cool.

Chop the red pepper into very thin strips. Chop the cabbage and Baby Gem into small strips and dice the spring onion, then add all of the veg to a large bowl.

Toast the seeds in a dry pan on a medium/high heat for a few minutes until toasted, then add them to the bowl.

Add the cooled quinoa to the bowl and mix everything well.

Make the dressing and then drizzle it into the bowl and toss together well.

GRILLED PEACH AND GOAT'S CHEESE SALAD

GF

SERVES 4 AS A STARTER, 2 AS A MAIN

100 g (3½ oz) mixed leaves (rocket, lamb's lettuce, chicory etc)

25 g (1 oz) beetroot or pea shoots

3 ripe peaches

1 tablespoon olive oil or truffle oil

50 g (2 oz) goat's cheese

For the dressing:

2 tablespoons balsamic vinegar

3 tablespoons olive oil

1 tablespoon honey

Pictured overleaf

There's nothing quite like a gorgeously ripe peach as it starts to caramelize and soften on the grill, and paired with some creamy goat's cheese, it's absolutely out of this world. You won't believe how good this salad is – you simply must try it. If peaches are out of season, use nectarines instead.

Combine the leaves and shoots in a large bowl.

Combine all of the dressing ingredients and whisk well. Drizzle onto the greens, tossing well.

Cut your peaches into wedges and drizzle with a little olive or truffle oil. Add them to a chargrill pan on a medium/high heat and cook for about 3 minutes until you have gorgeous char lines. Flip and repeat with the other side.

Crumble the goat's cheese over the greens. Arrange your warm grilled peaches on top and serve.

CHARGRILLED AVOCADO AND BEETROOT SALAD WITH PINE NUTS AND FETA

GF

SERVES 4

1 beetroot

2 avocados

1 tablespoon olive oil

35 g (1¼ oz/¼ cup) pine nuts

50 g (2 oz) lamb's lettuce or rocket

50 g (2 oz) feta, roughly chopped or crumbled

For the dressing:

2 tablespoons balsamic vinegar

3 tablespoons olive oil

1 tablespoon honey

1 teaspoon Dijon mustard

pinch of coarse salt and pepper

This is a spin on the classic beetroot and goat's cheese salad. The flavours are so incredible with the crunchy toasted pine nuts, crumbly feta and charred avocado all tossed in a sticky balsamic dressing.

Peel the beetroot and use a mandolin grater to slice it into paper-thin discs.

Put a chargrill pan on a high heat.

Remove the pit and skin from the avocados and cut them into thick wedges. Drizzle on a little bit of olive oil. Add them to the chargrill pan and cook for a few minutes each side, until you have dark char lines on both sides.

While the avocado is cooking, add the pine nuts to a dry pan on a medium heat and let them toast for a few minutes until golden brown.

Place the leaves and the beets in the serving dish and scatter over the feta. When the avocados are ready, arrange them on top and then sprinkle over the toasted pine nuts.

Combine all of the dressing ingredients and whisk well. Drizzle on the dressing and serve.

MAINS

VEGAN CHILLI

SERVES 4

2 sweet potatoes

2 tablespoons olive oil

1 teaspoon ground cumin

1 teaspoon ground cinnamon

1 teaspoon cayenne pepper

1 onion, diced

2 red or yellow peppers, deeseded and chopped

½ red chilli, deseeded and chopped

1 x 400 g (14 oz) tin chickpeas, drained

1 x 400 g (14 oz) tin kidney or butter beans, drained

2 x 400 g (14 oz) tins tomatoes

1 large handful of fresh coriander

coarse salt and pepper

OPTIONAL: Greek yoghurt

Talk about comfort food. This vegan chilli warms the soul – it's made for curling up by the fire with a bowl in your lap. This is the ultimate hearty winter dinner, full of yummy chickpeas, kidney beans and sweet potato. Perfect for coming home to after a wintery walk.

Preheat the oven to 200°C/400°F/Gas mark 6.

Peel and chop the sweet potatoes into small cubes. Add them to a roasting tray and drizzle them with a little olive oil and a sprinkle of salt and pepper before popping in the oven for about 30 minutes.

While they're cooking, add the olive oil to a large pot on a medium heat, followed by the spices. Let them toast and sizzle a bit and then add the onion, peppers and chilli to the pot.

Cook for 5–10 minutes until the onion and peppers have softened. Add in the chickpeas and beans and toss well, then add in the tinned tomatoes, stirring well. Let the chilli simmer and reduce for about 30 minutes.

When the sweet potatoes are ready, add them to the pot and give it a stir. Let the chilli cook for at least another 5 minutes after adding the sweet potatoes. The longer the flavours can infuse, the better.

Serve topped with fresh coriander and Greek yoghurt, if desired.

BUCKWHEAT MUSHROOM 'RISOTTO'

GF **DF** **V**

SERVES 4

175 ml (6 fl oz/¾ cup) boiling water

20 g (¾ oz) dried porcini mushrooms

4 tablespoons olive oil

1 white onion, diced

3 sprigs of fresh thyme

180 g (6 oz/1 cup) buckwheat groats

1 litre (1¾ pints/4 cups) chicken or vegetable stock

125 ml (4 fl oz/½ cup) almond milk, unsweetened

100 g (3½ oz) wild mushrooms

1 large handful of fresh parsley, roughly chopped

OPTIONAL TO SERVE:
Parmesan and truffle shavings

Sometimes nothing will do other than a piping hot, decadent bowl of comforting risotto – and this is so perfect. Here dried porcini mushrooms and fresh wild mushrooms are paired with with fragrant fresh thyme for a luxurious and creamy faux risotto. For extra wow, sprinkle with grated truffle shavings before serving.

Pour the boiling water over the dried mushrooms and let them soak for about 20 minutes.

Add 3 tablespoons of the olive oil to a large pan on a medium heat and add in the onion and the leaves of two sprigs of the thyme. Cook until the onion is soft and translucent.

Drain the dried mushrooms, keeping their soaking water and adding it to your stock. Add the dried mushrooms and buckwheat to the pan and stir until mixed together.

Pour in about a sixth of the stock/mushroom water mixture and let everything simmer until the liquid is almost all absorbed. Then keep repeating in similar amounts until all of the stock is used up. When almost all of the liquid is absorbed, add in the almond milk and mix well.

While the buckwheat is cooking, add a tablespoon of olive oil to a pan on a medium heat. Pinch the thyme leaves from the remaining stalk, then add the thyme leaves and fresh mushrooms to the pan and sauté for about 4 minutes. Unless the mushrooms are very large there is no need to chop them.

Cook your risotto until your desired wetness and then place the fresh mushrooms on top and serve. Sprinkle parsley on each serving, adding Parmesan and truffle shavings if desired.

BALSAMIC ROASTED ROOT VEGETABLES WITH POACHED EGGS

GF **DF** **P**

SERVES 2

2 sweet potatoes

2–4 carrots

2 parsnips

1 red onion

2 tablespoons olive oil

2 tablespoons balsamic vinegar

2 stalks of rosemary

4 eggs

2 tablespoons mixed seeds (pumpkin, sunflower, sesame, etc)

coarse salt and pepper

This is the best kind of end-of-the-week meal – when there's nothing left in the fridge apart from eggs and odd vegetables. You can use whatever vegetables you like (or have!) but the ones mentioned below taste wonderful. The soft egg yolks act as a beautiful dressing for the balsamic-glazed root veg and the seeds add a scrumptious crunch.

Preheat the oven to 200°C/400°F/Gas mark 6.

Peel all of your vegetables. For the sweet potatoes, cut them into wedges, and for the carrots and parsnips cut them lengthways, in either quarters or halves depending on size. Peel the red onion and cut it in half, then quarter the halves.

Add the veg to a roasting tray and drizzle the olive oil and balsamic all over them. Pinch the rosemary leaves from their stalks and sprinkle them all over, along with a generous pinch of coarse salt and pepper. Toss everything well with your hands. Pop them in the oven for about 45 minutes until crispy and browned.

A few minutes before the vegetables are ready, poach your eggs (page 12). While the eggs are on, toast your seeds in a dry pan on a medium/high heat for a few minutes until plump and delicious.

Take out the vegetables and divide them between your two plates. Place two poached eggs on top of each and then sprinkle on the toasted seeds. Season with salt and pepper as desired and serve.

CAJUN SALMON BURGERS

MAKES 6

½ large onion

400 g (14 oz) fresh salmon

1 egg

30 g (1 oz/¼ cup) ground almonds

2 teaspoons paprika

1 teaspoon cayenne pepper

1 teaspoon garlic powder

½ teaspoon ground cumin

juice of 1 lime, plus extra to serve

coconut oil, for frying

iceberg lettuce, to serve

coarse salt

These are so satisfying. The blend of spices is insanely yum and the zesty lime takes to salmon so perfectly. These quickly became a weekly occurrence in my house and once you try them you'll know why.

Chop the onion and salmon fillets into a few big chunks and add them to your food processor. Add in the egg, ground almonds, all of the spices, salt and lime juice too.

Pulse it a few times until everything is broken up and comes together. It should be a bit mushy, but still have some chunks (don't overblend).

Lay out a sheet of parchment paper on the counter and then wet your hands. Use your damp hands to shape the mixture into patties, laying them out on the parchment paper.

Heat a pan on a high heat and add a little coconut oil. When it's hot, add the burgers and cook for 4–5 minutes on each side.

Serve wrapped in fresh crunchy iceberg leaves with a generous squeeze of extra lime.

QUINOA NASI GORENG

GF **DF**

SERVES 2

2 tablespoons coconut oil

2 red peppers, deseeded and sliced

3–4 spring onions, chopped diagonally

½ red chilli, deseeded and finely chopped

150 g (5 oz) prawns

300 g (10½ oz/2 cups) cooked quinoa (page 10)

2 eggs

For the curry paste:

2 garlic cloves, minced

1 tablespoon tomato paste

1 teaspoon curry powder

2 tablespoons sesame oil

This recipe was born in a stubborn attempt to win my boyfriend over to Team Quinoa. It was certainly successful as he now loves quinoa (almost) as much as me and this recipe has been a blog favourite for the last few years. There is such joy in making an utterly simple meal that tastes unreasonably delicious for such little effort. With some leftover quinoa you can have this on the table in a matter of minutes. It tastes great with added chicken or pork, and for a yummy vegan dish just leave out the prawns and the egg.

In a bowl, mix together the minced garlic, tomato paste, curry powder and sesame oil.

Add half the coconut oil to a pan on a medium/high heat. When it's melted, add in about half of the curry paste and spread it around the pan. Add in the red pepper, spring onion, chilli and prawns and toss them around in the spices.

Let it all sizzle away for a few minutes until the pepper has started to soften. When the prawns are pink and plump, add in the cooked quinoa and the rest of the curry paste. Toss it all around, coating everything in the curry paste. Cook until the quinoa is heated through.

Add everything to your serving bowl/dish and leave the pan on the heat. Add the remaining coconut oil to the pan and crack your eggs straight in. Fry them to your liking and then pop one on top of each serving and serve straight away.

BUTTERNUT SQUASH AND SAGE COURGETTI

SERVES 2

500 g (1 lb 2 oz) butternut squash

2 garlic cloves

1 handful of fresh sage

1 tablespoon olive oil

2 courgettes

2 tablespoons pine nuts

60 ml (2 fl oz/¼ cup) almond milk

coarse salt and pepper

Butternut squash and sage are perfectly suited. For this recipe, I've roasted them with whole garlic cloves and olive oil before puréeing them into a gorgeous creamy pasta sauce bursting with heartwarming flavours. The sauce is served hot so it ever so slightly softens the raw courgetti to the perfect texture. Top with toasted pine nuts and some salt and pepper and you've got yourself the dreamiest bowl of courgetti goodness.

Preheat the oven to 200°C/400°F/Gas mark 6.

Remove the skin from the squash and chop it into cubes.

Add the squash to a roasting tray with the garlic cloves (leave them whole, skin on). Finely chop the sage leaves and sprinkle them over the squash with a good pinch of salt and pepper. Drizzle over the olive oil and toss together. Roast for about 30 minutes, until the squash is soft and starting to crisp.

While the squash is cooking, spiralize your courgettes and add to a large bowl. Toast the pine nuts in a dry pan on a medium heat for a few minutes until golden brown and set them aside.

Take the squash out and add three-quarters of it to your food processor. Squeeze the garlic from its skin and add that in along with the almond milk. Blend until smooth.

Pour the squash mixture into a saucepan and warm it up over a medium heat until hot.

Add your spiralized courgette to your serving bowl and top with the hot butternut squash sauce. Top with the reserved squash and pine nuts, season with salt and pepper and serve.

SESAME LIME STEAK SALAD

**SERVES 2 AS A MAIN,
4 AS A SIDE**

400 g (14 oz) steak

2 garlic cloves, minced

juice of 2 limes

coconut oil, for frying

1 tablespoon honey

1 tablespoon sesame seeds

3 tablespoons tamari

2 spring onions,
chopped diagonally

½ red chilli, finely sliced

120 g (4 oz) bean sprouts

1 handful of cashews

100 g (3½ oz) spinach

3 sprigs of fresh mint

coarse salt and pepper

This is pretty perfect and gorgeously zingy with a little bit of heat and a lovely crunch. The lime and fresh mint will soon make this a go-to lunch or dinner when you're craving something clean and refreshing in a hurry.

Place your steak in a bowl or dish. Sprinkle the garlic over the steak. Pour in the juice of 1 lime, sprinkle with coarse salt and pepper and then mix everything together well. Ideally, leave this to marinate for a few hours. Otherwise, set it aside while you get everything else ready.

Heat a pan on a high heat and add a little coconut oil. When the pan is hot, add in the steak.

Cook the steak for about 4 minutes on one side, then flip it over. After you've flipped it, drizzle the honey over the steak and sprinkle on the sesame seeds. When the steak is cooked to your liking, take it off the heat and set aside to rest.

Leave the pan on and turn the heat down to medium. Combine the tamari and the juice of 1 lime and set aside.

Add the spring onions, chilli, bean sprouts and cashews to the pan and then drizzle in the tamari/lime mixture. Cook for a few minutes, stirring regularly, until the cashews are golden brown and the bean sprouts have softened.

Add the spinach to a large bowl or plate, followed by the bean sprout mixture.

Slice the steak in thin diagonal pieces and place on top. Roughly chop the mint leaves and sprinkle on before serving.

GOOD KARMA KORMA

GF **DF** **P**

SERVES 2-4

2 tablespoons coconut oil

½ teaspoon cayenne pepper

½ teaspoon ground coriander

1 teaspoon ground turmeric

1 teaspoon garam masala

1 white onion, diced

1 aubergine, chopped into cubes

300 g (10½ oz) chicken breast, chopped into cubes

3 garlic cloves, minced

1 teaspoon fresh ginger, grated

4 tablespoons ground almonds

4 tablespoons desiccated coconut

1 x 400 ml (14 fl oz) tin coconut milk

To serve:

fresh coriander, flaked almonds

This is real comfort food at its best. Korma is mild, but bursting with flavour and full of subtlety. The aubergine absorbs the flavour beautifully and really compliments the sweetness of the ground almonds and coconut that I use for thickness and flavour. It also tastes great if you want to keep it vegan. Just add in some sweet potato or squash instead of the chicken to bulk it up.

Add the coconut oil to a pot on a medium heat. When it's melted, sprinkle in all of the spices. Let them heat up until they start to sizzle.

Add the onion, aubergine and chicken to the pot and stir them, making sure everything is coated in the spices. Pop the lid on and let them cook away for about 5 minutes, stirring occasionally.

Add in the garlic and grated ginger and toss again. Pop the lid back on for another 5 minutes until the aubergine is soft.

Add the ground almonds and desiccated coconut to your food processor and blitz on high until fine.

Add the coconut milk to the pot and turn the heat up until it starts to simmer. Add in the coconut almond mixture and stir well, then let the curry simmer and reduce for about 15 minutes.

Serve with some fresh coriander leaves and a sprinkle of flaked almonds.

SOPHIE'S CHICKEN KIEV

GF **DF** **P**

SERVES 2

2 large garlic cloves, very finely crushed

15 g (½ oz) fresh parsley leaves, finely chopped

15 g (½ oz) fresh basil leaves, finely chopped

2 slices of prosciutto, finely chopped

60 g (2 oz/½ cup) ground almonds

45 g (1½ oz/½ cup) desiccated coconut

1 egg

2 chicken breasts

coconut oil, for frying

coarse salt and pepper

This is one recipe I simply couldn't leave out. It's a huge hit on my blog and also one of my personal favourites. Named after my big sister Sophie, who persistently pestered me to Little Green Spoon-ify one of her favourite dinners, it's everything you love about the classic, but with a few cleaner twists.

Preheat the oven to 180°C/350°F/Gas mark 4.

Start by making your filling. Add the garlic, herbs and prosciutto to a bowl and mash with a fork, making sure everything is evenly mixed together.

Add the ground almonds and desiccated coconut to another bowl and mix them together.

Whisk your egg in a separate bowl. Season your chicken with salt and pepper and then cut a small pocket in the centre of the chicken, but don't cut all the way through to the other side.

Stuff your filling neatly into the pocket and close it over so that nothing is spilling out.

Use one hand to dip the chicken carefully into the egg to coat it, letting any excess drip off. Then use the other hand to dip it into the almond/coconut mixture to coat.

Heat a little coconut oil in a pan on a medium heat. Add the chicken and let them sizzle for about 2 minutes on each side until they are nice and golden, then pop them in the oven for about 15 minutes until cooked through and crispy.

BALSAMIC AND SAGE ROAST CHICKEN

GF **DF** **P**

SERVES 4

5 stalks of fresh sage

5 tablespoons olive oil

4 tablespoons balsamic vinegar

3 garlic cloves, minced

1.75 kg (4 lb) whole chicken

5 carrots

5 parsnips

2 white onions

1 lemon

coarse salt and pepper

Although most people love a classic lemon and thyme-stuffed chicken, sometimes you want something extra special, and this is just that. Sage is absolutely heavenly with balsamic and garlic. The chicken is so succulent and has amazing juices, which make the vegetables taste fantastic and act as an instant gravy.

Preheat the oven to 180°C/350°F/Gas mark 4.

Remove most of the sage leaves from the stalks and finely chop them, keeping back one or two stalks with the leaves still on. Add the chopped sage to a bowl with the olive oil, balsamic vinegar, garlic and a good pinch of coarse salt and pepper. Stir everything around.

Place the chicken in your roasting tray. Peel the carrots and parsnips and chop them in half lengthways. Slice one of the onions into wedges and one into thin half rings (these taste amazing in the gravy) and position all of the vegetables tightly around the chicken.

Cut the lemon in half and push it into the chicken cavity, along with the remaining sage stalks.

Lift the skin around the cavity and use your hands to squeeze some of the balsamic sage rub between the chicken breast and its skin – you want a thin layer under all of the top skin. Spoon the rest over the top of the chicken, making sure the entire chicken has been covered in the gorgeous flavours. Pour any excess over the vegetables. Sprinkle everything with coarse salt and pepper.

Pop the tray in the oven and roast for 80–90 minutes. About halfway through, poke the chicken and let the juices run into the tray, then baste the chicken with the juices and toss the vegetables. The chicken is cooked when you can easily pull the thigh meat away from the bone and the juices run clear.

When it's cooked, there should be lots of delicious juices in the roasting tray. While removing the chicken from the tray, tilt it over the tray for a few seconds to allow any extra juices to drizzle from the chicken into the tray, then plate your vegetables and pour all of the juices into a jug for incredible instant gravy!

ALMOND CHICKEN SATAY

GF **DF** **P**

SERVES 4

4 chicken breasts

1 teaspoon ground turmeric

1 teaspoon ground ginger

1 teaspoon ground coriander

1 tablespoon melted coconut oil

2 garlic cloves, minced

1 tablespoon coconut oil

For the satay sauce:

200 ml (7 fl oz/¾ cup) coconut milk

2 tablespoons almond butter

juice of 1 lime

YOU WILL NEED:
metal or wooden skewers (if using wooden skewers, soak in water for at least 30 minutes before using)

Satay is a funny one for me – being allergic to peanuts, I've never tried the real thing! That's not to say I haven't lusted after it for years. Every time somebody beside me ordered it, I knew I would love it, if only I could taste it. So with a lot of research into the perfect satay sauce and a lot of help from taste testers, I finally came up with a me-friendly version, and boy was it worth the wait. This recipe is everything I always hoped satay would be, and it's so simple! A satay lover's dream and any peanut allergy sufferer's fantasy.

Cut the chicken breasts into chunks and slide them onto the skewers.

Combine the turmeric, ground ginger, ground coriander, melted coconut oil and garlic. Coat the chicken in the paste. If you have time, cover and leave to marinate for at least an hour (and up to 24 hours). Otherwise, move on to the next step.

Whisk together the coconut milk and almond butter in a pan on a medium/high heat and bring it to a simmer. Add the lime juice and let it simmer and thicken for about 10 minutes, adjusting the heat if necessary.

As the sauce thickens, heat a chargrill pan on a medium/high heat and add the tablespoon of coconut oil. When it's melted and hot, add the chicken skewers. Cook for a few minutes each side until you have gorgeous char lines and the chicken is cooked through.

Plate the chicken skewers and serve with the sauce drizzled on top, with extra on the side.

CHICKEN AND BROCCOLI BAKE

GF **DF** **P**

SERVES 4

coconut oil, for frying

300 g (10½ oz)
mushrooms, chopped

250 ml (8½ fl oz/1 cup)
coconut milk

250 ml (8½ fl oz/1 cup)
chicken stock

1 teaspoon mustard
powder

400 g (14 oz)
chicken breasts

300 g (10½ oz) broccoli

100 g (3½ oz/¾ cup)
hazelnuts

coarse salt and pepper

OPTIONAL: cheese

Chicken and broccoli bake is classic comfort food. It's the perfect dinner and makes lovely leftovers. This is a great recipe to have in your repertoire as it actually warms the soul and is surprisingly simple to make. It's also really easy to double or make in bulk, so it can feed a crowd. If you make too much, it freezes really well, too.

Preheat the oven to 180°C/350°F/Gas mark 4.

Heat a teaspoon of coconut oil in a large saucepan on a medium heat, then add in the mushrooms. Sprinkle with salt and pepper and cook until they start to grey and soften – about 5 minutes.

Pour in the coconut milk and chicken stock and stir, then take it off the heat and sprinkle in the mustard powder. Use a handheld food processor to blitz it until as smooth as possible (or just pour it into your food processor), then set it aside.

Heat about a tablespoon of coconut oil in a pan on a medium/high heat while you chop the chicken and the broccoli into little pieces. Add them to the pan and cook for about 5 minutes until the broccoli is bright green and the chicken is almost fully cooked.

While they're cooking, add the hazelnuts to your food processor and blitz until you have a breadcrumb-like consistency. Then add in ½ tablespoon melted coconut oil and some salt and pepper and blitz again until you have a fluffy, crumbly mixture.

Add the chicken and broccoli to your casserole dish, then pour the mushroom sauce over it and mix well.

Sprinkle the hazelnut mixture and the cheese, if using, generously over the top.

Pop it in the oven for 40 minutes.

To reheat leftovers, just pop it back in the oven until heated through. To freeze, let it cool completely before wrapping in foil and freezing. When serving, let it defrost for a few hours, then cook until heated through.

COD GOUJONS

GF **DF**

SERVES 2

225 g (8 oz/1¾ cups) chickpea/gram flour

2 teaspoons baking powder

200 ml (7 fl oz/¾ cup) fizzy water

200 g (7 oz) cod

1 tablespoon coconut oil

lemon, for squeezing

coarse salt and pepper

This batter is so light and crispy and, sprinkled with a little salt and a good squeeze of lemon, it's just perfection. It's hard to believe how easy these are to make – they'll quickly become a favourite.

Combine 200 g (7 oz/1½ cups) of the chickpea/gram flour, the baking powder, fizzy water and some salt and pepper in a bowl and whisk well. Add the remaining flour to a different bowl.

Cut the cod into fingers.

Dip the cod lightly in the plain chickpea/gram flour and then in the batter to coat.

Heat the coconut oil in a pan on a high heat. When it's really hot, add the first goujon and repeat the above steps with the rest.

Cook for a few minutes on each side until crispy and golden on both sides and cooked through.

Serve with a squeeze of fresh lemon.

ROAST SWEET POTATO CURRY

GF **DF** **P** **V**

SERVES 4

3 small sweet potatoes

3 tablespoons tomato paste

2 teaspoons garam masala

1 teaspoon ground cumin

½ teaspoon ground ginger

½ teaspoon cayenne pepper

2 garlic cloves, minced

2 tablespoons coconut oil

1 large white onion, diced

400 g (14 oz) chicken or 2 aubergines (v)

600 ml (1 pint/2½ cups) chicken or vegetable stock (v)

This is one of the best dinners on a rainy day. It makes the kitchen smell amazing and is like a hug in a bowl. Add chicken if you wish or stick with aubergine as a vegan option. This recipe has a lovely medium heat, but you can reduce or leave out the cayenne for a milder curry. Serve with some fluffy quinoa, Mango Chutney (page 125) and Raita (page 128).

Preheat the oven to 200°C/400°F/Gas mark 6.

Start by peeling and cubing the sweet potatoes. When the oven is hot, add them to a roasting tray, with no oil, and roast for about 30 minutes.

When they have been in for about 15 minutes, toss them.

Mix the tomato paste, spices and garlic in a bowl.

Add the coconut oil to a pot on a medium heat. When it's melted, add in the curry paste and let it sizzle for a minute.

Add in the diced onion and stir, coating the onion in all of the spices. Let the onion soften while you chop the chicken (or aubergines) into small chunks.

Add the chicken (or aubergines) in and stir everything around, then pop the lid on. Let everything steam for about 2 minutes and then stir again and repeat for another 2 minutes.

The sweet potatoes should be ready by now. Take them out of the oven and add them straight to the pot, tossing everything together. Pour in your stock and stir. Turn up the heat to bring the curry to a boil, then turn the heat back down to medium and let everything simmer away, reducing and thickening, for 20–25 minutes before serving.

BEST-EVER CHARGRILLED CHICKEN

GF

SERVES 4

2 teaspoons paprika

½ teaspoon cayenne pepper (a little more if you want more heat!)

½ teaspoon ground cumin

¼ teaspoon ground cinnamon

1 garlic clove, minced

3 tablespoons olive oil, plus extra for frying

3 tablespoons Greek yoghurt

juice of 1 lemon

4 chicken breasts

This is one of the most popular recipes on my blog and my absolute favourite way to eat chicken. Drenched in gorgeous Middle-Eastern spices and charred for extra flavour; it's incredible with everything.

Combine all of the marinade ingredients in a bowl.

Lay your chicken out on a sheet of parchment paper and use the back of a spoon to spread half of the mixture evenly over the breasts. Flip them over and do the same with the rest of the marinade. Place another sheet of parchment paper on top of the chicken breasts and pound them with a rolling pin until tender and thin. If you have time, cover the chicken and pop it in the fridge for up to 24 hours to let it marinate in the gorgeous spices. If not, you can cook it straight away.

Heat a chargrill pan on a high heat (or even better, use a barbecue!) and drizzle on a little olive oil. When it's hot, add the chicken breasts. Let them cook for about 6 minutes on each side, until cooked through and gorgeously charred.

PISTACHIO AND ROSEMARY-CRUSTED LAMB CUTLETS

SERVES 2

3 stalks of fresh rosemary

75 g (2½ oz/½ cup) pistachios

1 garlic clove, peeled

4–6 lamb cutlets

1 tablespoon olive oil

4 teaspoons Dijon mustard

coarse salt and pepper

If you only try one recipe in this book, let it be this. It is one of those dishes that words can't describe – it's crazy delicious. You'll be licking the plate and chasing every last bit of pistachio crust off it. This is a great one for dinner parties as it has a real wow factor, but is surprisingly easy and amazing every time.

Preheat the oven to 200°C/400°F/Gas mark 6.

Remove the rosemary leaves from their stalks and add them to your food processor with the pistachios and garlic. Blend until the pistachios and rosemary are broken down into a fine crumble, then add the mixture to a bowl.

Season the lamb cutlets with a little salt and pepper. Heat a pan on a medium/high heat and add in the olive oil. Add the lamb cutlets and cook for about 2 minutes on each side until browned.

Take the lamb out of the pan and use a butter knife to spread about a teaspoon of mustard onto one side of each cutlet in a thin layer, then dredge in the pistachio mixture.

Place the lamb cutlets, crust side up, on a roasting tray and roast for about 10 minutes until cooked through.

TERIYAKI MEATBALLS

GF **DF**

SERVES 4

400 g (14 oz) pork mince

2 spring onions,
finely chopped

2 eggs, whisked

5 tablespoons ground
almonds

5 tablespoons tamari

2 tablespoons honey

1 tablespoon coconut oil

These are such a crowd pleaser! Everyone dies for the sticky glaze. My mom used to make these for us all the time as kids and I still love them just as much as I did then. You can serve them with almost anything, but I love to make some extra sauce and have them with quinoa and a crunchy salad or slaw.

Preheat the oven to 200°C/400°F/Gas mark 6.

Add the mince to a large bowl and break it up with your fingers.

Add the spring onions to the mince with the whisked eggs and ground almonds. Use your hands to mix everything together really well.

In a separate bowl, combine the tamari and honey and whisk it well.

Pour about two-thirds of the sauce into the meatball mixture and work everything together with your hands.

Wet your hands and shape the mixture into balls, I like to make mine about the size of a golf ball.

Heat a pan on a medium/high heat and add the coconut oil. When it's melted and the pan is hot, add the meatballs and cook them on each side until they're nice and crispy.

Take them off the heat and add them to a baking sheet. Drizzle the remaining sauce all over them and cook for about 12 minutes until cooked through.

BEEF PHO

GF **DF**

SERVES 4

For the broth:

2 large onions,
cut into quarters

1 thumb-sized piece of
fresh ginger, peeled

2 cinnamon sticks

3 star anise

3 cloves

1 teaspoon coriander seeds

2 litres (3½ pints)
beef stock

1 tablespoon tamari

150 g (5 oz) soba
buckwheat noodles

To serve:

1 courgette

400 g (14 oz) steak

100 g (3½ oz) bean sprouts

3 spring onions, diced

1 handful of fresh coriander,
roughly chopped

1 lime, cut into wedges

A good pho is one of the best, most comforting meals there is. The broth is like no other – simultaneously rich and light. This is a simplified, really quick version – perfect for making at home in a hurry. There are lots of spices to give the broth flavour without taking hours, and the mixture of buckwheat noodles and fresh spiralized courgettes makes it lovely and light and adds a pretty pop of colour. All of the toppings are super refreshing and it's just divine with a good squeeze of lime. If you're in the mood, add in a boiled egg at the end, too.

Place the onions and ginger in a large pot on a medium/high heat and cook until charred on both sides.

Turn the heat down to medium and add in all of the spices. Pour in the beef stock and tamari and let it gently simmer and reduce for about 30 minutes.

While it's cooking, spiralize the courgette and cut the steak into small, very thin strips.

When the broth is ready, strain it to remove the spices, onion and ginger and then return it to a pot on a medium heat. Bring the broth to a boil, add in the noodles and then adjust the heat down to a simmer. Cook the noodles for about 5 minutes.

Divide the spiralized courgette into your bowls and top with the raw steak slices.

Pour the very hot broth in on top to fill the bowls. This will cook the steak and soften the courgette noodles. Make sure the steak is submerged in the broth.

Serve and let everybody add their desired amounts of bean sprouts, spring onions, coriander and lime.

SWEET POTATO AND BUTTERNUT SQUASH SHEPHERD'S PIE

GF **DF** **P**

SERVES 4

2 tablespoons olive oil

1 large onion, diced

3 medium carrots, chopped

4 sprigs of fresh thyme

500 g (1 lb 2 oz) lamb mince

2 tablespoons tomato paste

400 ml (13 fl oz/1½ cups) beef stock

400 g (14 oz) sweet potatoes

400 g (14 oz) butternut squash

3 garlic cloves

coarse salt and pepper

Anything with layers usually seems like a lot of hassle, but this really isn't. It's not the fastest dish to make, but it is really simple, makes great leftovers and is perfect for freezing. It's topped with puréed butternut squash, sweet potato and garlic mash and the fresh thyme in the filling brings even more flavour. This is autumn comfort food at its best.

Preheat the oven to 180°C/350°F/Gas mark 4.

Heat a tablespoon of olive oil in a pan on a medium heat and add in the onion and carrots. Add the fresh thyme leaves to the pan and cook for about 6 minutes until the onion and carrots have softened.

Turn the heat up a little and add in the lamb mince. Use your spatula to break up the meat and stir everything around. Let the lamb cook for about 5 minutes until browned.

Transfer the lamb mixture to your baking dish. Add the tomato paste to your beef stock, stir well and then pour it over the meat. Season with a good pinch of salt and pepper. Cover with foil and cook for about an hour.

While that's cooking, put a large pot of water on a medium/high heat and bring it to a boil. While it's heating up, peel the sweet potatoes and quarter them. When the water is boiling, turn the heat down a little to a simmer and add in the sweet potatoes. Let them cook on their own for about 5 minutes.

Recipe continued overleaf

While the sweet potatoes are on, peel and chop the squash into chunks. Peel the garlic cloves and bash them with the palm of your hand. Add the squash and garlic to the pot and cook until the squash and sweet potatoes are tender when pierced with a fork.

When the sweet potatoes and squash are done, drain them and then add them back to the pot with about a tablespoon of olive oil and a good pinch of salt. Use a potato masher to mash them until smooth and creamy. Then set aside.

When the meat is ready, take it out and turn the oven temperature up to 200°C/400°F/Gas mark 6. Spread the sweet potato-squash mash over the top of the meat. Season with a good pinch of salt and pepper and bake for 20–25 minutes until the top starts to crisp and the meat bubbles around the edges. Serve straight away.

To freeze, leave it to cool completely before wrapping in foil and freezing. When serving, leave it to defrost, then cook in the oven at 200°C/400°F/Gas mark 6 until heated through.

SESAME CHICKEN FINGERS

 GF **DF** **P**

SERVES 4

60 g (2 oz/½ cup)
ground almonds

35 g (1¼ oz/¼ cup)
sesame seeds

1 tablespoon melted
coconut oil

1 egg, whisked

400 g (14 oz) chicken breast

coarse salt

Who knew chicken nuggets could be good for you? A little more gourmet than chicken nuggets, I'll admit, but crispy and succulent and great for you – these are perfect for kids and make an ideal cravings buster! For a real treat, dip them into some Garlic Mayo (page 132).

Preheat the oven to 200°C/400°F/Gas mark 6.

Combine the ground almonds, sesame seeds and salt in a bowl. In a separate bowl, combine the melted coconut oil and whisked egg.

Cut your chicken into finger-sized pieces. Use one hand to dip a piece of chicken into the egg, then use the other hand to dip it into the almond-sesame mixture. Using separate hands will stop the mixtures clumping. Repeat with each piece of chicken.

Lay the chicken out on a baking sheet lined with parchment paper and cook for 25–30 minutes until golden brown. Flip them after about 20 minutes.

BREAD

OLIVE AND ROSEMARY BREAD

GF **DF** **P**

MAKES 1 LOAF

5 stalks of fresh rosemary

60 g (2 oz) olives, pitted

3 eggs

3 tablespoons olive oil, plus extra for greasing

280 g (10 oz/2⅓ cups) ground almonds

1 teaspoon baking powder

1 teaspoon coarse salt

The classic Mediterranean pairing of rosemary and olives taste particularly fantastic together in bread. This loaf develops a lovely crispy top while the inside stays soft and pillowy – perfect for soaking up sauces! Serve as is or toasted.

Preheat the oven to 170°C/325°F/Gas mark 3.

To start, pinch the rosemary stalks with your fingers and run your fingers down the stalks to remove the leaves. Set a few aside for decorating at the end. Finely chop the rest and roughly chop the olives into little chunks.

In a large bowl, combine the eggs and olive oil.

In a separate bowl, combine the ground almonds, baking powder, salt and chopped rosemary.

Add the egg mixture into the almond mixture and mix until well combined, then fold in the olives. You should have a thick, mushy mixture.

Spread the mixture into a 1lb loaf tin greased with a little olive oil and use a spatula or the back of a spoon to spread the top out evenly, trying to get it as smooth as possible. Sprinkle the top with some more fresh rosemary and the coarse salt for decoration.

Bake for about 35 minutes until a knife inserted into the middle comes out clean. Let the bread cool on a wire rack before slicing and serving.

QUINOA TORTILLAS

GF **DF** **V**

MAKES 6

200 g (7 oz/2 cups)
quinoa flour, plus extra
for dusting

180 ml (6 fl oz/¾ cup)
water

60 ml (2 fl oz/¼ cup)
olive oil

These are a revelation! This was one of the hardest recipes I've ever worked on. It took me days and endless amounts of quinoa flour (and possibly a few tantrums!) to get this right. In the end I finally got it, with just three simple ingredients! They were so worth the trouble – everything you love about regular tortillas, but with a subtle hint of the nutty flavour and all of the nutritional punch of quinoa. These are great for breakfast, lunch or dinner and you can use them exactly as you would regular tortillas. Hallelujah!

Combine the quinoa flour, water and olive oil in a large bowl.

Use your hands to squeeze and knead it all together until a sticky ball of dough forms. Keep kneading it until you have a smooth ball. It may be a little sticky, but you should be able to move it between your hands without it sticking to them.

Divide the dough in half, then divide each half in three and roll the six chunks into balls. They should feel light and soft.

Lay some parchment paper out on a chopping board and lightly dust it with quinoa flour. Put one of the balls in the centre and sprinkle a little more flour over it. Use a rolling pin to roll the dough into a very thin circle. Add more flour if it starts to stick and roll as thin as you can without it breaking.

Heat a pan on a high heat. Peel the tortilla carefully from the parchment paper and add it to the pan. Cook for about 90 seconds on both sides.

Repeat with the remaining balls.

If keeping for later, leave to cool completely then wrap tightly in foil and store in the fridge for up to 3 days. Reheat in a pan.

SWEET POTATO BREAD

GF **DF**

MAKES 1 LOAF

300 g (10½ oz) sweet potato

2 eggs

60 ml (2 fl oz/¼ cup)
olive oil, plus extra
for greasing

185 g (6½ oz/1½ cups)
buckwheat flour

1 teaspoon baking powder

pinch of coarse salt

This bread is neither sweet nor savoury, yet perfectly in between. The soft sweet potato purée makes it moreishly bouncy with a slight sweetness and its versatility knows no bounds. It tastes awesome whether it's slathered with almond butter or dunked in soup.

Preheat the oven to 180°C/350°F/Gas mark 4.

Boil a large pot of water. Peel and chop the sweet potatoes into cubes. Add them to the pot of boiling water and boil until tender when pricked with a fork, about 15 minutes.

Drain the sweet potatoes, add them to your food processor and blend until smooth.

Let the purée cool a little, then add it to a large bowl and whisk it together with the eggs and olive oil.

In a separate bowl, combine the buckwheat flour, baking powder and salt.

Add the dry ingredients into the sweet potato mixture gradually, mixing well.

Pour the mixture into a 1lb loaf tin greased with a little olive oil and bake for 30–35 minutes until a knife inserted into the middle comes out clean.

BLUEBERRY BANANA BREAD

MAKES 1 LOAF

4 bananas

3 eggs

60 ml (2 fl oz/¼ cup) melted coconut oil, plus extra for greasing

1 tablespoon vanilla essence

3 tablespoons honey/ maple syrup

300 g (10½ oz/2½ cups) ground almonds

1 teaspoon baking powder

1 teaspoon ground cinnamon

100 g (3½ oz/¾ cup) blueberries

Banana bread brings contentment like nothing else. From the smell that fills the kitchen to the taste of the very last crumb. This is made with a hint of cinnamon speckled through it and plump blueberries bursting out. You can also add in dark chocolate chips instead.

Preheat the oven to 170°C/325°F/Gas mark 3.

Start by mashing your bananas with a fork. Add the mashed banana, eggs, coconut oil, vanilla and sweetener to a large bowl and mix.

In a separate bowl, combine the ground almonds, baking powder and cinnamon and mix it all together. Then gradually add the dry ingredients to the wet, mixing it all well. Fold in the blueberries.

Grease a 1lb loaf tin with a little coconut oil. Pour the mixture into the tin and bake for about 55 minutes, until a knife inserted into the middle comes out clean.

DADDY BREAD

GF **DF** **V**

150 g (5 oz/1½ cups)
gluten-free oats (to be
made into oat flour)

200 g (7 oz/2 cups)
gluten-free oats

130 g (4½ oz/1 cup)
chickpea/gram flour

100 g (3½ oz/¾ cup)
sunflower seeds, plus extra
to sprinkle (optional)

100 g (3½ oz/¾ cup)
pumpkin seeds, plus extra
to sprinkle (optional)

2 teaspoons bicarbonate
of soda

750 ml (1⅓ pints/3 cups)
almond milk, unsweetened

2 tablespoons apple
cider vinegar

2 tablespoons maple syrup

coconut oil, for greasing

3 tablespoons sesame seeds

For as long as I can remember, my dad has been making this bread, which is kind of a miracle because he doesn't cook – at all. Having said that, Daddy Bread (as we call it) is everybody's favourite, from the doorman in my sister's office to the local doctor in a little village in France. Once based on a traditional Irish soda bread recipe, it's morphed over the years into something quite unique. It's a little bit different every time, depending on what he has to hand. It always reminds me of home and every bite is filled with love. It's especially good hot out of the toaster with almond butter and mashed banana.

Preheat the oven to 190°C/375°F/Gas mark 5.

Add the 150g of gluten-free oats to your food processor and blend until you have a fine oat flour. Add it to a large bowl.

Add the whole gluten-free oats to the bowl with the chickpea gram flour, sunflower seeds, pumpkin seeds and bicarbonate of soda. Mix everything together really well.

Combine the almond milk and apple cider vinegar in a bowl. Pour it into the dry ingredients gradually, while stirring.

Pour in the maple syrup, while stirring, and mix until you have quite a wet, gloopy mixture.

Grease a 1lb loaf tin with a little coconut oil. Pour the mixture into your tin, then sprinkle generously with sesame seeds. You can also sprinkle on some pumpkin or sunflower seeds.

Bake for about 95 minutes until the bread feels hard to the touch and when you insert a knife, it comes out clean.

Store in the fridge in an airtight container for up to a week.

BERRY BUCKWHEAT SCONES

GF **DF**

MAKES 12

300 g (10½ oz/2½ cups) buckwheat flour, plus extra for dusting

180 g (6 oz/1½ cups) ground almonds

1½ teaspoons baking powder

125 ml (4 fl oz/½ cup) melted coconut oil

2 eggs

125 ml (4 fl oz/½ cup) maple syrup/honey

75 g (2½ oz/½ cup) blueberries

75 g (2½ oz/½ cup) raspberries

Scones demand rolling and cutting, but fear not – the effort's worth it and these ones couldn't be simpler. These are made with a combination of buckwheat flour and ground almonds for a crumbly centre and the berries make them look pretty and keep them moist while adding a bit of zing.

Preheat the oven to 180°C/350°F/Gas mark 4.

Combine the buckwheat flour, ground almonds and baking powder in a large bowl.

Pour in the melted coconut oil gradually, while mixing, until you have a grainy mixture.

In a separate bowl, combine the eggs and sweetener and mix well. Pour into the buckwheat mixture and mix well.

Mix in the blueberries and raspberries and use your hands to shape the dough into a ball, then divide the ball in two.

Lightly dust a flat surface with buckwheat flour and use a rolling pin to roll out one dough ball until it's about an inch thick. The scones won't rise that much so you want them cut nice and thick.

Use a 6 cm (2.5 in) round pastry cutter to cut the dough into scones and lay them out on a baking tray lined with parchment paper. Repeat with the second ball of dough.

Bake for about 17 minutes until they're golden brown on top and the blueberries are bursting out.

Serve warm from the oven. To reheat, pop them in the oven at 180°C/350°F/Gas mark 4 until heated through.

LEMON AND POPPY SEED DRIZZLE LOAF

GF **DF** **P**

MAKES 1 LOAF

80 ml (2½ fl oz/⅓ cup) melted coconut oil, plus extra for greasing

180 ml (6 fl oz/¾ cup) honey

150 ml (5 fl oz/⅔ cup) almond milk

zest of 2 lemons

2 tablespoons poppy seeds

300 g (10½ oz/2½ cups) ground almonds

2 teaspoons baking powder

½ teaspoon coarse salt

2 egg whites

For the drizzle:

1 x 400 ml (13 fl oz) tin coconut milk, refrigerated overnight

2 tablespoons honey

juice of 2 lemons

To serve:

lemon peel

This loaf is virtuously light, gorgeously zesty and sports the most delicious drizzle of frosting – what's not to love? Heaven with a cup of tea.

Preheat the oven to 180°C/350°F/Gas mark 4.

In a large bowl, combine the melted coconut oil, honey, almond milk, lemon zest and poppy seeds. Keep the lemons that you zested, you can use their juice for the drizzle.

In a separate bowl, combine the ground almonds, baking powder and salt.

Gradually add the almond mixture to the wet ingredients in three stages, mixing well after each addition.

In a separate bowl, whisk the egg whites until stiff peaks form, then gently fold the egg whites into the batter.

Grease a 1lb loaf tin with coconut oil or line it with parchment paper. Pour the mixture into the tin and bake for 35–40 minutes until golden on top and a knife inserted into the middle comes out clean.

As soon as you put the loaf in the oven, make the drizzle. Scoop the coconut cream from the top of the tin of chilled coconut milk (keep the coconut water for something else). Add it to a large bowl and mix in the honey and lemon juice. You should have a tart, runny mixture. Pop it in the fridge to thicken just a little while the loaf cooks.

Take out the loaf and leave it to cool. When the loaf is completely cool, take the drizzle out of the fridge, give it a stir and then spoon it on to the loaf, letting it drip down the sides. Top with strips of lemon peel.

DOUBLE CHOCOLATE
PECAN BREAD

GF **DF** **P**

MAKES 1 LOAF

4 eggs

60 ml (2 fl oz/¼ cup) melted coconut oil, plus extra for greasing

125 ml (4 fl oz/½ cup) maple syrup

100 g (3½ oz/1 cup) pecans

180 g (6 oz/1½ cups) ground almonds

4 tablespoons cacao powder

1 teaspoon baking powder

pinch of coarse salt

90 g (3¼ oz/½ cup) dark chocolate chips

Chocolate. Bread. Need I say more? This is such a crowd pleaser and it really is as good as it sounds. Enjoy it by itself or with loads of different toppings. Try mashed banana or it's also amazing with almond butter – anything goes!

Preheat the oven to 180°C/350°F/Gas mark 4.

Combine the eggs, melted coconut oil and maple syrup in a large bowl.

Add the pecans to a food processor and blend on high until the pecans are ground as fine as you can get them.

Combine the ground almonds, ground pecans, cacao powder, baking powder, salt and chocolate chips and mix well.

Gradually add the dry ingredients into the wet and mix well.

Grease a 1lb loaf tin with a little coconut oil and then pour the whole mixture in.

Bake for 40–45 minutes until a knife inserted into the middle comes out clean (ignore any melted chocolate chips). Best served warm.

SAUCES, DIPS AND SPREADS

SUN-DRIED TOMATO AND PISTACHIO PESTO

GF **DF** **V** **P**

MAKES 1 X 200 ML (7 FL OZ) JAR

75 g (2½ oz/½ cup) pistachios

75 g (2½ oz/½ cup) sun-dried tomatoes

25 g (1 oz) basil

2 garlic cloves

80 ml (2½ fl oz/⅓ cup) olive oil

pinch of coarse salt

This will soon become your favourite pesto. Marry roasted pistachios with sun-dried tomatoes and basil and you've got a winner. You can use this on courgetti, in salad dressings, as a marinade or a dip.

Preheat the oven to 180°C/350°F/Gas mark 4.

Dry roast the pistachios for 10 minutes.

While they're in the oven, roughly chop the sun-dried tomatoes and basil and mince the garlic. Add them to your food processor with the olive oil and blend until you have a chunky paste.

Add in the pistachios and a pinch of coarse salt and blend until the pistachios are mostly broken down. I like to have some very fine and some chunky.

Store in an airtight jar in the fridge for up to 2 weeks.

HEALTHY HOLLANDAISE

GF **DF** **P**

SERVES 2

juice of ½ lemon

2 egg yolks

3 tablespoons coconut oil

coarse salt

Hollandaise is such a treat. It's silky and luxurious and can elevate even the humblest of ingredients into something sensational. This one is creamy and smooth, but wonderfully light. Drizzle it over asparagus or salmon and, of course, drown a poached egg in it on a Sunday morning.

Fill your blender with boiling water and put the lid on. This will heat the blender and help cook the egg yolks.

Combine the lemon juice and egg yolks in a bowl.

Pour out the water from the blender and pat it dry quickly, then pour in the yolks and lemon juice and blend until combined.

Melt your coconut oil and, while it's still warm, pour it very slowly into the blender on low power, you will see it thicken with each addition. Sprinkle in some salt, blend to combine and then serve.

ASIAN CITRUS DRESSING

**MAKES 125 ML
(4 FL OZ/½ CUP)**

juice of 2 limes

juice of 1 lemon

4 tablespoons tamari

3 tablespoons olive oil

1 garlic clove, minced

This has a lot more oomph than more traditional dressings and also works well as a light dipping sauce or marinade. It makes an amazing dip for the Quinoa Sushi (page 155).

Combine all of the ingredients and whisk well.

Serve straight away or whisk well again before serving.

MANGO CHUTNEY

GF **DF** **V** **P**

MAKES 400 G (14 OZ)

1 tablespoon coconut oil

1 teaspoon nigella seeds

½ teaspoon mustard seeds

½ teaspoon ground cumin

½ teaspoon ground ginger

½ teaspoon ground coriander

1 garlic clove, minced

1 white onion, diced

450 g (1 lb) mango flesh, chopped into small chunks

125 ml (4 fl oz/½ cup) apple cider vinegar

250 ml (8½ fl oz/1 cup) honey/agave

Mango chutney is in a league of its own. It's not only amazing served in the traditional way with Indian dishes, but it also dresses up other savoury dishes. Add it to dressings and mayo and use it as a marinade for chicken, too. This one has loads of delicious spices, which add so much flavour, and it's so easy to make – just leave it to bubble away until it's ready.

Add the coconut oil to a large pot on a medium heat. When it's melted, add in all of the spices and let them sizzle for a minute.

Add in the garlic and onion and toss everything well. Let them cook for 2–3 minutes until they start to soften, stirring regularly.

Add the mango, vinegar and sweetener to the pot and stir well. Turn the heat up and bring it to a boil, then turn down the heat to medium/low and let it simmer for about 60 minutes. You can just leave it to bubble away with no attention needed, but keep an eye on it towards the end as you may need to turn down the heat for the last few minutes.

You can either leave it nice and chunky (I do!) or mash it with a potato masher for a smoother chutney.

Store in an airtight jar in the fridge for up to 2 months.

GARLIC, CHILLI AND TURMERIC HUMMUS

GF **DF** **V**

**MAKES 400 G
(14 OZ/2 CUPS)**

240 g (8½ oz) chickpeas, soaked or tinned

2 tablespoons tahini

juice of ½ lemon

2 garlic cloves, minced

¼ red chilli

1 teaspoon ground turmeric

pinch of coarse salt

3 tablespoons olive oil

The hummus to end all hummuses. Using spices and fresh herbs adds flavour and colour to dips and this and the Beetroot Hummus with Roasted Pistachios and Coriander (page 133) will have you eating the rainbow ... and licking the bowl!

Drain the chickpeas and add them to the food processor with the tahini, lemon juice, garlic, chilli, turmeric and salt. Blend until smooth, making sure the chilli is well blended.

While blending on low, gradually pour in the olive oil. Blend until smooth and creamy.

RAITA

GF

**MAKES 250 G
(9 OZ/1 CUP)**

240 g (8½ oz/1 cup)
Greek yoghurt

1 teaspoon ground cumin

20 g (¾ oz) fresh mint,
roughly chopped

½ large cucumber

coarse salt

When the going gets hot, cool and refreshing mint and cucumber in soft, creamy yoghurt is the answer. It's also a delicious dip and is superb mixed into mushy peas, if you're so inclined.

Add the Greek yoghurt, cumin, pinch of salt and the mint to the food processor and blitz until the mint is really finely broken down. Pour into your serving bowl.

Grate the cucumber in on top and mix well.

Serve cold.

LEMON VINAIGRETTE

**MAKES 125 ML
(4 FL OZ/½ CUP)**

juice of 2 lemons

3 tablespoons olive oil

1 teaspoon Dijon mustard

1 garlic clove, minced

coarse salt and pepper

Light, zingy and fresh – this will become your go-to salad dressing. It complements all kinds of leaves, is so delicious tossed through quinoa and also makes an awesome marinade for chicken. If you're short on time and want an instant, fresh hit of flavour, make this ahead of time and keep it in a little jar in the fridge – just give it a good shake and drizzle it on. Save spice jars for transporting it on the go.

Combine the lemon juice, olive oil, Dijon mustard and garlic and whisk well.

Add a good pinch of coarse salt and pepper to taste.

Whisk well before serving.

PERFECT GUACAMOLE

SERVES 4

2 large ripe avocados

¼ large red onion, diced

10 g (½ oz) fresh coriander, finely chopped

2 garlic cloves, minced

juice of 1 lime

coarse salt and pepper

Perfect guacamole is hard to come by, but this one's pretty perfect. A lovely crunch from the red onion, tang from the coriander and just the right amount of garlic and lime. It's just like they serve it in Mexico and is good with everything. It will keep for a few days in the fridge in an airtight jar or container. Just pour a thin layer of water over the top, then put the lid on and pop it in the fridge – this will stop it browning. When serving, drain off as much of the water as you can, give it a good mix and it will be good as new.

Cut your avocados in half, remove the pit, scoop the flesh from the skin and add it to a large bowl. Add in the onion, coriander, garlic, lime juice and a good pinch of coarse salt and pepper.

Mash everything together with a fork so it's chunky/smooth to your liking. Taste and add more salt, pepper or lime to your liking.

Serve straight away or store as suggested above.

GARLIC MAYO

**MAKES 250 ML
(8½ FL OZ/1 CUP)**

2 egg yolks

3 teaspoons lemon juice/
red wine vinegar

125 ml (4 fl oz/½ cup)
melted coconut oil

125 ml (4 fl oz/½ cup)
olive oil

pinch of coarse salt

2 garlic cloves, minced

Garlic mayo is so versatile and tastes good no matter what you dunk in it. You can use this recipe, with or without the garlic, to make loads of different flavours of mayo, too. Just add pesto, mustard, spices, even Mango Chutney (page 125).

Add the egg yolks and lemon juice/vinegar to a food processor and blend until combined.

Combine the oils, then very slowly and gradually add the oil to the egg mixture on a low speed. This is very important and it should take a few minutes for you to pour in all of the oil. You'll notice it thicken with each addition and when all of the oil has been added, it should be thick and glossy.

Add in the salt and minced garlic and blend until combined.

Store the mayo in the fridge in an airtight container. Due to the coconut oil it will solidify in the cold. Take it out of the fridge prior to eating to allow it to soften, and whisk before serving.

BEETROOT HUMMUS WITH ROASTED PISTACHIOS AND CORIANDER

MAKES 400 G (14 OZ/2 CUPS)

1 handful of pistachios

240 g (8½ oz) chickpeas, soaked or tinned

2 beetroots, boiled and chopped into small chunks

2 tablespoons tahini

juice of ½ lemon

pinch of coarse salt

1 garlic clove, minced

3 tablespoons olive oil

1 small handful of fresh coriander

To serve:

fresh crudités

Pictured overleaf

This is the prettiest dip. Iron-rich beetroot makes this hummus taste amazing and look outrageously pink, while the pistachios and fresh coriander speckle it with bright green and even more flavour. This tastes and looks fabulous with almost anything and will be the star of any meal.

Preheat the oven to 180°C/350°F/Gas mark 4.

Roast the pistachios for 8–10 minutes. While they're cooking, make the hummus.

Drain your chickpeas and add them to the food processor with the beetroot, tahini, lemon juice, salt and garlic. Blend until smooth.

While blending on low, gradually add in the olive oil until smooth and creamy.

Transfer the hummus to your serving bowl and sprinkle on the roasted pistachios and fresh coriander.

MIXED BERRY CHIA JAM

**MAKES 330 G
(11 OZ/1 CUP)**

100 g (3½ oz/¾ cup)
strawberries

100 g (3½ oz/¾ cup)
raspberries

100 g (3½ oz/¾ cup)
blackberries

2 tablespoons honey/
maple syrup

2 tablespoons chia seeds

The easiest jam you'll ever make. No bubbling, stirring or waiting, just some beautiful berries, a little natural sweetener and some clever chia seeds. The chia seeds swell in the berry juices, gradually thickening the gorgeous jam into the perfect consistency. You can use just one type of berry or as many as you can find. This combination is perfectly sweet and beautifully tart.

Remove the green tops from the strawberries and add them to your food processor with the raspberries and blackberries. Blend until smooth.

Add in the sweetener and blend until combined. Taste for sweetness and add more if needed, this will depend on how ripe your berries are.

Add in the chia seeds and blend. Let it rest for a few minutes to allow the chia seeds to swell and thicken, then blend again.

Store in an airtight jar in the fridge for about a week.

CHOCOLATE CASHEW BUTTER

MAKES 1 X 250 ML (8½ FL OZ) JAR

300 g (10½ oz/2 cups) cashews

2 tablespoons cacao powder

3 tablespoons maple syrup/honey

This is such a treat! Cashew butter is the king of all nut butters – it's thicker and creamier and when you add in chocolate? Sublime.

Preheat the oven to 180°C/350°F/Gas mark 4.

Roast the cashews for about 8 minutes, until golden brown and fragrant.

Add them straight to the food processor and blitz until ground. Then add in the cacao powder and sweetener.

Blitz on high until you've reached your desired runniness. This should take about 10 minutes depending on your blender. The mixture will become doughy, then it will roll into a ball and then finally start to liquify. Don't lose faith – just keep blending!

HOT CHOCOLATE SAUCE

SERVES 4

75 ml (2½ fl oz/⅓ cup) coconut milk

1 tablespoon honey/ maple syrup

75 g (2½ oz) dark chocolate

coarse salt

The fudgeyness of this chocolate sauce is insane. Drizzle it over a scoop of dairy-free ice cream or simply dip in some fresh strawberries or bananas for the most luxurious treat.

Add the coconut milk and sweetener to a saucepan on a medium/low heat.

Chop the chocolate into chunks and add it to the saucepan with a pinch of coarse salt.

Let it melt slowly, whisking gently, until you have a glossy, smooth chocolate sauce.

PECAN PIE SPREAD

**MAKES 1 X 250 ML
(8½ FL OZ) JAR**

300 g (10½ oz/
2½ cups) pecans

4 tablespoons maple syrup

The name says it all! This tastes exactly like pecan pie and is so easy to make. Spread it on bread, dunk a banana in or lick it straight off the spoon!

Preheat the oven to 180°C/350°F/Gas mark 4.

Add the pecans to a bowl and drizzle over the maple syrup. Toss everything around so that the pecans are evenly coated.

Spread the pecans out on a baking tray and roast for about 8 minutes.

Add the hot maple pecans to your food processor and blend on high for a few minutes, stopping to scrape down the sides as needed. The amount of time this takes will depend on how powerful your machine is. If it's taking a long time, don't lose faith, just keep blending!

When you've reached your desired runniness, store in an airtight jar in the fridge for up to 3 months.

ON
THE GO

CHILLI LIME KALE CHIPS

SERVES 1

100 g (3½ oz) kale

1 tablespoon olive oil

¼ teaspoon cayenne pepper

zest of 2 limes

½ teaspoon coarse salt

These kale chips are so crisp and satisfying, cooked with a little cayenne to generate a bit of heat and then tossed in lime salt for the most amazing zing! Kale chips often get soggy if not eaten straight away: store them in a container filled with a little rice – the rice will absorb any excess moisture and keep the kale chips crisp for up to 2 days. Just pop them in a bag with some rice for the perfect grab-and-go snack for work, school or a picnic.

Preheat the oven to 150°C/300°F/Gas mark 2. Line a roasting tray with parchment paper.

Remove the kale leaves from the stalks and add them to your tray. Drizzle on the olive oil and use your hands to mix it all around and massage the kale for about 2 minutes. This is so important as it gives the chips a much better texture. Sprinkle on the cayenne and toss well.

Roast for about 20 minutes until crisp.

While the kale is cooking, add the lime zest to a bowl with the salt. Mix well.

When the kale chips are done, add them to a large bowl and sprinkle on the lime salt, tossing well.

Let the chips cool completely before adding them to your bag or container.

PROTEIN POWER POT

GF **DF**

SERVES 1

1 egg

1 tablespoon mixed seeds (sunflower, sesame, pumpkin, etc)

85 g (3 oz/½ cup) leftover cooked quinoa (page 10)

½ avocado, pit and skin removed

1 tablespoon chopped fresh chives

1 teaspoon olive oil

1 handful of spinach

½ lemon

coarse salt and pepper

It can be hard to pack savoury things in advance that will still taste great by the time you eat them, so stick to fresh, simple ingredients that are delicious in their own right. This combination is so yummy and is packed with protein and healthy fats – no heating or sauce required, just a quick squeeze of lemon juice and you're good to go.

Add your egg to a pot of boiling water and boil for about 8 minutes so that it is perfectly between soft and hard.

While the egg is boiling, add your seeds to a dry pan on a medium heat and cook for a few minutes until toasted and delicious.

Add the cooked quinoa to a bowl with the avocado and chives. Peel your egg and add it to the bowl. Drizzle in the olive oil and a little salt and pepper and use a fork and knife to chop and mash everything together.

Add the spinach to your container, followed by the quinoa/egg mixture. Sprinkle on the seeds. Slice the lemon into wedges and place them on top.

When it's time to eat, squeeze on the lemon and grab a fork!

TRUSTY TRAIL MIX

GF **DF** **V** **P**

MAKES 8–10 SERVINGS

50 g (2 oz/⅓ cup) almonds

50 g (2 oz/⅓ cup) cashews

35 g (1¼ oz/⅓ cup) pecans

25 g (¾ oz/⅓ cup)
coconut chips

3 tablespoons seeds
(pumpkin, sunflower,
chia, sesame, etc)

½ teaspoon ground
cinnamon

35 g (1¼ oz/¼ cup) dried
cherries or cranberries

Trail mix is nothing new, but a few really simple moves can take it to the next level. This combination is so delicious and makes the best snack or porridge topping. It's called a 'Trusty' trail mix because it tastes amazing no matter what you have it with. Store in a big jar and snack on it by the handful or pack it into little bags for snacking on the go.

Preheat the oven to 180°C/350°F/Gas mark 4.

Combine the almonds, cashews, pecans, coconut chips and seeds in a large bowl. Add in the cinnamon and mix well. Spread the mix out onto a roasting tray and roast in the oven for about 10 minutes.

Take the tray out of the oven and mix in the dried fruit. Leave it to cool completely before storing in an airtight jar for up to 1 month.

CREAMY SESAME NOODLES

GF **DF** **V**

SERVES 2-4

2 large courgettes

1 red pepper

2 tablespoons sesame seeds

For the dressing:

65 g (2¼ oz/¼ cup) tahini

3 tablespoons tamari

2 tablespoons red
wine vinegar

2 tablespoons honey/agave

1 tablespoon sesame oil

juice of 1 lime

This is a really reliable, lightning-fast recipe that always works. It is ready in under 5 minutes and served cold, so it tastes amazing straight away or as leftovers from the fridge. It has the perfect sauce-to-noodle ratio with a scrumptiously nutty, creamy dressing and a yummy little crunch from the sesame seeds. Destined to be lunchbox inspo, it's the ideal office lunch if you make it the night before.

Spiralize the courgettes and add them to a large bowl. Deseed the pepper, slice into really thin strips and add to the bowl.

Add the sesame seeds to a dry pan on a medium heat and let them toast away while you make the dressing. Toss them every minute or so. They are done when you start to hear popping.

Add all of the dressing ingredients to a bowl and whisk well until you have a creamy, smooth mixture.

Pour the dressing over the courgettes and toss, coating everything evenly. Sprinkle the sesame seeds on top and serve.

BLUEBERRY CRUMBLE MUFFINS

GF **DF**

MAKES 10

130 ml (4½ fl oz/½ cup) softened coconut oil

200g (7 oz/1⅓ cups) coconut sugar

2 eggs

1 teaspoon vanilla essence

200 g (7 oz/2 cups) gluten-free oats

1½ teaspoons baking powder

½ teaspoon ground cinnamon

120 ml (4 fl oz/½ cup) almond milk

100 g (3½ oz/¾ cup) blueberries

For the topping:

2 tablespoons gluten-free oats

2 tablespoons coconut sugar

Whether you're having breakfast at your desk or sipping on a leisurely cup of tea, these are sure to hit the spot. The coconut sugar topping makes them gorgeously crisp on top while the inside is perfectly crumbly and bursting with sweet blueberries.

Preheat the oven to 180°C/350°F/Gas mark 4. Line a 12-hole muffin tin with muffin cases.

Use an electric mixer to whisk the softened coconut oil until it's smooth. Add in the coconut sugar and whisk until you have an even, grainy mixture.

Add in the eggs, one at a time, whisking well, and then add the vanilla.

Add the oats to your food processor and blitz on high until you have a fine oat flour, then add in the baking powder and cinnamon and pulse to combine.

Add half of the oat flour mixture to the egg mixture, followed by half of the almond milk. Mix well and then repeat with the rest of the oat flour and almond milk.

Fold in the blueberries.

Pour the mixture into your muffin cases. Combine the oats and the coconut sugar for the topping and sprinkle some on top of each muffin.

Bake for 15–20 minutes until a knife inserted into the middle comes out clean.

CHOCOLATE HAZELNUT PROTEIN BALLS

GF **DF** **V** **P**

MAKES 8–10

150 g (5 oz/1 cup) pitted dates

150 g (5 oz/1 cup) hazelnuts

1 scoop of vanilla protein powder (I use Sunwarrior)

1 tablespoon cacao powder

These are one of the most moreish snacks – just try scooping a bit of the crumbly roasted hazelnut, cacao and date mixture straight from the food processor! You can roll the balls whatever size you like. If you go for quite a large golf ball-size, you'll get a few bites worth.

Preheat the oven to 180°C/350°F/Gas mark 4.

Pour boiling water over the dates and let them soak for at least 5 minutes.

Dry roast the hazelnuts for about 10 minutes. When they're done, rub them around in a clean kitchen towel to remove any loose shells.

Add the hazelnuts to the food processor and blend until broken down into a coarse, crumbly nut flour. Add in the protein and cacao powders and blend to combine.

Drain the dates and add them in, blending on high until you have a sticky paste.

Use your hands to shape the mixture into balls.

Store in an airtight container for up to 2 weeks.

CRUNCHY OAT BARS

GF **DF** **V**

MAKES 9

150 g (5 oz/1½ cups) gluten-free oats

45 g (1½ oz/½ cup) desiccated coconut

½ teaspoon baking powder

4 tablespoons coconut oil

75 g (2½ oz/½ cup) coconut sugar

1 teaspoon vanilla essence

pinch of coarse salt

Deliciously crunchy, these will sate even the rumbliest tummy, young or old. The ideal after-school treat.

Add the oats, desiccated coconut and baking powder to a large bowl.

Add the coconut oil, coconut sugar and vanilla to a saucepan on a medium heat and let it melt until thick and glossy, whisking frequently. Take off the heat and stir in a pinch of coarse salt.

Pour the wet ingredients into the dry ingredients and mix really well.

Line a 23 cm (9 in) baking tin with parchment paper and pour the oat mixture in, pressing it firmly into the tin. Make sure to press it all the way into the corners.

Bake for about 15 minutes until golden brown.

Let the mixture cool for about 20 minutes before carefully chopping it into bars, then let them cool entirely and crisp up.

QUINOA SUSHI

GF **DF** **V**

MAKES 4 ROLLS

170 g (6 oz/1 cup) quinoa

500 ml (17 fl oz/2 cups)
vegetable stock

assorted vegetables
(avocado, cucumber,
spring onion, enoki
mushrooms, beetroot, etc)

4 sheets of nori

OPTIONAL: wasabi,
pickled ginger, tamari

YOU WILL NEED:
a sushi rolling mat

This recipe borrows the general idea of sushi to make a simple veggie quinoa version for a clever portable lunch. You can use whatever vegetables you like, but do try avocado, cucumber, spring onion, enoki mushrooms and a little bit of beetroot for some brightness. Serve with a mountain of pickled ginger.

Cook your quinoa in the vegetable stock until light and fluffy (page 10) and then set it aside to cool.

Prepare and chop your vegetables into thin strips.

Lay one of the nori sheets onto your sushi mat, with the rough side up and the faint lines horizontal so that they're parallel to the bottom of the mat. Use your fingers to press a quarter of the warm quinoa into the nori, right to the bottom edge and the sides, about three-quarters of the way up. You want a tightly pressed, thin layer of quinoa. Using warm quinoa makes it easier to squish, but make sure it's not hot or the nori will go soft.

If using wasabi, add a little bit in a line about a centimetre from the bottom. Lay out the vegetables in a line on top of the wasabi.

Roll the sushi mat forward over itself, pulling tightly, then roll again. Keep doing this until you reach the end. Make sure to tighten as you roll.

Repeat with the rest of your rolls. Then chop each one into individual pieces.

Store in an airtight container in the fridge until serving or taking with you. Serve with pickled ginger and/or tamari.

DATE AND NUT BARS: TWO WAYS

MAKES 8

150 g (5 oz/1 cup)
pitted dates

150 g (5 oz/1 cup) cashews

**For the cacao and
orange bars:**

zest of 1 large orange

2 tablespoons cacao powder

OR

**For the coconut and
vanilla bars:**

4 tablespoons
desiccated coconut

1 teaspoon vanilla powder

These are the simplest and yummiest little snacks. Both flavours have just four ingredients, but so much flavour! The cacao and orange ones taste like such a treat with the fresh orange zest speckled throughout the rich cacao powder; they're also full of powerful antioxidants and minerals from the raw cacao. The vanilla ones are slightly crumblier and a little sweeter.

Add the dates to a bowl and pour boiling water over them. Leave them to soak and soften for about 10 minutes.

Add the cashews to your food processor and blitz until you have a coarse, bitty mixture. You want them really broken down but still with a few chunks.

To make the cacao and orange bars, add the zest and cacao powder to the cashew mixture. Blend to combine.

To make the coconut and vanilla bars, add the desiccated coconut and the vanilla powder to the ground cashews. Blend until combined.

Drain the dates and add them to the food processor. Blend on high until everything is completely combined and you have a sticky, crumbly paste.

Line a 20 cm (8 in) baking tin with parchment paper and press the mixture into the tin. It doesn't matter if the mixture doesn't fill the tin, just press it into a square.

Pop it in the fridge for about half an hour and then chop into bars or squares. They'll keep for up to 2 weeks in the fridge in an airtight container or for about 3 days in the cupboard.

ALMOND BUTTER PROTEIN BALLS

MAKES 8–10

150 g (5 oz/1 cup) almonds

150 g (5 oz/1 cup) pitted dates

1 scoop of vanilla protein powder (I use Sunwarrior)

65 g (2¼ oz/¼ cup) almond butter

OPTIONAL: cacao powder, desiccated coconut, nuts, etc

Pictured overleaf

Roasted almonds and vanilla protein bound together with sticky dates and almond butter – these are a little too good. It's so hard to stop at one! These are a great snack, whether you need a pick-me-up after the gym or a little afternoon treat with a cup of tea.

Preheat the oven to 180°C/350°F/Gas mark 4.

Roast the almonds for about 10 minutes until fragrant and delicious.

While they're roasting, soak the dates in boiling water.

Add the almonds to your food processor and blend until you have a chunky flour. Add in the protein powder and blend to combine.

Add in the drained dates and almond butter and blitz on high until you have a sticky paste.

Use your hands to roll the mixture into balls and roll in any of the optional extras, if you like.

Store in an airtight container for up to 2 weeks.

SUPER SNACK BARS

MAKES 12

150 g (5 oz/1 cup) pitted dates

100 g (3½ oz/1 cup) gluten-free oats

50 g (2 oz/½ cup) flaked almonds

35 g (1¼ oz/¼ cup) seeds (pumpkin, sunflower, chia, sesame, etc)

1 teaspoon ground cinnamon

60 ml (2 fl oz/¼ cup) melted coconut oil

These super snack bars are perfect for grabbing for a breakfast on the go or beating the afternoon lull. Packed full of oats and super seeds, one of these is just what you need to give you that extra push through the day. They're chewy and licky, sticky good so you'll be fighting the urge not to stop at one.

Add the dates to a bowl and pour boiling water over them. Let them soak for about 10 minutes. While they're soaking, combine the oats, flaked almonds, seeds and cinnamon in a large bowl.

Add the dates and 2 tablespoons of their soaking water to your food processor and blitz on high until they are well broken up into a paste. Add in the coconut oil and blend some more until you have a smooth(ish!) mixture.

Pour the date mixture into the bowl with the dry ingredients and mix thoroughly.

Spread the mixture out into a 20 cm (8 in) baking tin lined with parchment paper and pop it in the freezer for about an hour. Take out, slice and serve!

Store in an airtight container for up to 2 weeks.

SESAME COFFEE BLISS BALLS

GF **DF** **V** **P**

150 g (5 oz/1 cup)
pitted dates

2 tablespoons instant coffee

150 g (5 oz/1 cup) almonds

2 tablespoons tahini

2 tablespoons sesame seeds

These. Are. Heaven. Soaking the dates in strong coffee infuses them with a faint flavour that works so well with the toasted sesame seed coating and rich tahini. They're quite literally the perfect afternoon slump pick-me-up and they keep really well for up to 2 weeks, so they're ideal for grabbing from the cupboard at the last minute. Keep a stash under your desk.

Preheat the oven to 180°C/350°F/Gas mark 4.

Add the dates and the instant coffee to a bowl. Pour boiling water over the dates, just enough to cover them, and leave them to soak.

Add the almonds to a roasting tray and roast for 10 minutes.

Add the roasted almonds to your food processor and blitz until broken down into a chunky flour.

Drain the dates, discarding the coffee, and add them to the food processor along with the tahini, blending until you have a sticky paste.

Add the sesame seeds to a dry pan on a medium/high heat and toast them until they start to pop.

Roll the date mixture into balls, then roll them in the toasted sesame seeds to coat.

Store in an airtight container for up to 2 weeks.

TREATS

CARROT CAKE

GF **DF** **P**

MAKES 1 TWO-TIER CAKE

For the cake:

4 eggs

375 ml (13 fl oz/1½ cups) melted coconut oil, plus extra for greasing

1 teaspoon vanilla essence

375 ml (13 fl oz/1½ cups) maple syrup/honey

480 g (1 lb 1 oz/4 cups) ground almonds

1½ teaspoons mixed spice

2 teaspoons baking powder

150 g (5 oz/1 cup) walnuts

400 g (14 oz) carrots, peeled and grated

For the icing:

2 x 400 ml (13 fl oz) tins coconut milk (kept in the fridge overnight)

60 ml (2 fl oz/¼ cup) honey

1 teaspoon vanilla essence

75 g (2½ oz/½ cup) walnuts

Carrot cake has a wonderful texture and complexity. Here chopped walnuts are folded into the cake batter for extra chew and the icing is made from whippy coconut cream for even more decadence.

Preheat the oven to 180°C/350°F/Gas mark 4.

Whisk the eggs, melted coconut oil, vanilla and sweetener.

In a separate bowl, combine the ground almonds, mixed spice and baking powder.

Gradually add the dry ingredients to the wet.

Roughly chop the walnuts and add them to the cake batter with the grated carrot. Mix well.

Grease two 20 cm (8 in) cake tins with a little coconut oil. Divide the mixture evenly between the two and bake for about 40 minutes, until a cake tester comes out clean. While the cakes are cooking, take the tins of coconut milk out of the fridge to allow them to soften a little.

Let the cakes cool completely, then make the icing.

Scoop the coconut cream from the top of the tins (keep the coconut water for something else). Add the cream to a large bowl and whisk it together with the honey and vanilla until you have a gorgeous whippy frosting. If you're not icing the cake straight away, keep the icing in the fridge until just before.

When the cakes are cooled, ice the bottom one then place the second cake on top. Then ice the top cake.

Finely chop the walnuts and sprinkle them on top. I like to toast the walnuts before for even more flavour.

ALMOND BUTTER SWIRL BROWNIES

GF DF P

MAKES 9–12

375 g (13 oz/1½ cups)
almond butter

250 ml (8½ fl oz/1 cup)
maple syrup

2 eggs

1 teaspoon vanilla extract

50 g (2 oz/½ cup)
cacao powder

1 teaspoon baking powder

big pinch of coarse salt

These are the best things ever! Fudgey, sticky, finger-licking brownies at their best, with sweet, creamy almond butter swirls and a smell that will bring the neighbours knocking. There's a lot of almond butter in here, which makes this recipe a little expensive, but it is totally worth it. These are last-meal-on-earth good.

Preheat the oven to 180°C/350°F/Gas mark 4.

Combine the almond butter and maple syrup in a large bowl (try not to eat it all, it's incredible!).

Separate and set aside about one-third of the mixture.

Add the eggs and vanilla to the remaining two-thirds.

Add in the cacao powder, baking powder and salt and mix thoroughly.

Line a 20 cm (8 in) baking tin with parchment paper and pour in the thick glossy mixture.

Scatter dollops of the remaining almond butter mixture all over and use a knife to run through it, marbling the mixture.

Bake for about 22 minutes depending on how you like them. I like mine fudgey and sticky so that's exactly how long I leave them in.

Leave them to cool for at least 10 minutes before slicing.

PISTACHIO TRUFFLES

GF **DF** **V** **P**

MAKES 4–6

150 g (5 oz/1 cup)
pistachios, unshelled,
plus extra to decorate
(optional)

1½ tablespoons melted
coconut oil

1 tablespoon maple
syrup/honey

pinch of coarse salt

75 g (2½ oz) dark chocolate

These home-made chocolates look so pretty and they taste incredible. They're the ideal after-dinner treat or thoughtful gift for someone special.

Preheat the oven to 180°C/350°F/Gas mark 4.

Dry roast the pistachios for 8–10 minutes. Add to your food processor and blitz on high until you have a bright green, chunky powder.

Drizzle in the coconut oil and sweetener and a pinch of salt and blitz on high for a full 90 seconds.

When you're done, melt your chocolate.

Squeeze and roll the mixture into little balls. If it feels too bitty, just squeeze it tightly together before rolling into a ball.

Dip each one into the chocolate, shaking off any excess. You can top each one with a few chopped pistachios, if you like. Set them on a plate or board covered in parchment paper and pop them in the fridge to set.

CARAMEL CASHEW CLUSTERS

GF DF V P

MAKES 6

75 g (2½ oz/½ cup) cashews

2 tablespoons cashew butter

2 tablespoons date syrup

75 g (2½ oz) dark chocolate

coarse salt

Crunchy roasted cashew clusters with a chewy, sticky caramel centre and a dark chocolate coating, topped with a sprinkling of sea salt. These are so simple to make and they're seriously addictive.

Preheat the oven to 180°C/350°F/Gas mark 4.

Add the cashews to a roasting tray and roast for about 8 minutes.

While they're roasting, combine the cashew butter and date syrup and mix well into a sticky caramel.

Melt your chocolate and set it aside.

On some parchment paper, arrange the cashews into clusters of about 6 to 8 nuts. Then add a dollop of the caramel on top of each cluster so that they stick together.

Drizzle a layer of melted chocolate over each and sprinkle with a little coarse salt.

Pop in the fridge to set before serving.

CHOCOLATE-DIPPED FIGS WITH SEA SALT

GF **DF** **V** **P**

SERVES 4

4 figs

50 g (2 oz) dark chocolate

½ teaspoon coconut oil

coarse sea salt

These are the simplest of after-dinner treats and are as delicious as they are pretty. They're perfect for entertaining as they require minimal effort and look fabulous. Use a really good-quality, high-percentage dark chocolate and perfectly ripe figs for a beautifully rich, guilt-free treat.

Use a very sharp knife to cut the figs lengthways into thin slivers. The rounder, outer two pieces of each fig might not contain enough flesh to bother coating, in which case just eat them while you prepare the chocolate!

Place your chocolate in a small bowl so that the melted chocolate is deep enough for dipping, and melt over, but not touching, a pan of boiling water. Stir in the coconut oil until melted and smooth. Line a board/plate with parchment paper.

Dip each fig slice in the chocolate about halfway up and then lay it out on the parchment paper. When all the slices are done, sprinkle a little sea salt over the chocolate and pop them in the fridge to set.

ROCKY ROAD

GF **DF** **V** **P**

MAKES 9-12

50 g (1¾ oz/⅓ cup)
hazelnuts

50 g (1¾ oz/⅓ cup)
pistachios

100 g (3½ oz/¾ cup)
pitted dates

185 ml (6¼ fl oz/¾ cup)
melted coconut oil

35 g (1¼ oz/⅓ cup)
cacao powder

75 g (2⅔ oz/⅔ cup)
Grain-Free Maple Pecan
Granola (page 25)

35 g (1¼ oz/⅓ cup)
dried apricots or other
dried fruit

Little cubes of nutty, crumbly, chewy heaven. I had to get
a bit creative to come up with textures that mirror traditional
rocky road, and although these might not be exactly the same,
they taste even better! Grain-Free Maple Pecan Granola (page
25) replaces biscuits, while toasted hazelnuts and pistachios
are added for crunch and dates for yummy chewiness. You
can sub or add in different nuts and dried fruit, if you like.

Preheat the oven to 180°C/350°F/Gas mark 4.

Dry roast the hazelnuts and pistachios for about 10 minutes,
until toasted and delicious. Put the dates in a bowl and pour
boiling water over them, leaving them to soak for about
10 minutes.

Add the drained dates to your food processor with the melted
coconut oil and cacao powder. Blend on high until smooth
(ish!) then transfer to a bowl.

Pour in the granola, apricots and nuts and mix well.

Spread the mixture into a 20 cm (8 in) baking tin lined with
parchment paper and pop in the freezer to set. When set,
chop into little squares.

Store in the fridge.

CARAMEL SQUARES

MAKES 8–10

For the base:

150 g (5 oz/1 cup)
pitted dates

150 g (5 oz/1 cup) cashews

For the caramel:

150 g (5 oz/1 cup)
pitted dates

125 g (4 oz/½ cup)
almond butter

60 ml (2 fl oz/¼ cup)
melted coconut oil

coarse salt

For the top layer:

120 g (4 oz) dark chocolate

If you're going to master one raw dessert, let it be this one. These squares are a complete classic and everybody who tries them can't get enough.

Place the dates for the two layers in two separate bowls and pour boiling water over them. Leave them to soak for about 10 minutes, then drain them.

Line a 20 cm (8 in) baking tin with parchment paper.

To make the base, place the cashews in the food processor and blend until you have a coarse flour. Add in one bowl of drained dates and blend on high until you have a smooth paste.

Press the mixture evenly into your baking tin. Then put it in the fridge while you make the caramel.

To make the caramel, blend the second bowl of drained dates until as smooth as your food processor will allow. Then add in the almond butter and melted coconut oil and blend to combine. You should get a thick glossy mixture.

Spread the caramel over the base layer, then pop the tin in the freezer for about an hour.

To finish, melt the chocolate and pour it over the caramel layer. Freeze for about 20 minutes or until set, then slice into squares.

Store in an airtight container in the fridge for up to a week, or in the freezer for a couple of months.

BANOFFEE JARS

SERVES 4

For the base:

75 g (2½ oz/½ cup) pitted dates

100 g (3½ oz/¾ cup) walnuts

For the middle:

2 bananas

2 tablespoons maple syrup/honey

2 tablespoons almond butter

For the top:

1 x 400 ml (13 fl oz) tin coconut milk (kept in the fridge overnight)

10 g (½ oz) dark chocolate

Desserts with layers may seem like they're a lot of effort, but you just need a food processor and a bowl for this one and you don't even have to clean the food processor in between layers. It has a walnut and date base, a sweet banana middle and it is topped with coconut cream and chocolate.

Preheat the oven to 180°C/350°F/Gas mark 4. Take the tin of coconut milk out of the fridge to soften a little.

Put the dates in a bowl and pour boiling water over them, leaving them to soak for about 10 minutes.

Add the walnuts to a roasting tray and pop them in the oven for 8–10 minutes until toasted and fragrant.

When the walnuts are ready, add them to your food processor and blend until you have a chunky, coarse flour. You don't want them too fine, just nice and crumbly.

Drain the dates and add them to the walnuts, blending well until evenly mixed together into a crumbly paste.

Divide the base mixture among your jars and press it firmly into the bottom of each.

Add the bananas, sweetener and almond butter to your food processor (no need to clean it between layers) and blend until you have a creamy mixture. Divide this among your jars.

Scoop the coconut cream from the chilled tin of coconut milk (keep the coconut water for something else). Add it to a bowl and whisk until smooth and creamy. Divide this among the jars.

Grate the chocolate in on top and serve. If making ahead of time, seal the jars and refrigerate until serving. They will last for up to 24 hours.

LITTLE CHOCOLATE
HAZELNUT TARTS

GF **DF** **V** **P**

MAKES 6

For the crust:

225 g (8 oz/1½ cups) hazelnuts, plus extra to garnish

60 g (2 oz/½ cup) ground almonds

3 tablespoons melted coconut oil

3 tablespoons maple syrup/honey

coarse salt

For the filling:

1 x 400 ml (13 fl oz) tin coconut milk (kept in the fridge overnight)

2 tablespoons cacao powder

75 ml (2½ fl oz/⅓ cup) maple syrup/honey

These need no introduction. They are a bite-sized dream.

Preheat the oven to 180°C/350°F/Gas mark 4. Take the tin of coconut milk out of the fridge, setting it aside to soften a little.

Roast the hazelnuts for 8–10 minutes until they start to brown.

Let them cool and then rub them in a kitchen towel to remove any loose shells. Add them to your food processor with the ground almonds and blend until you have a fine flour.

Add in the melted coconut oil, sweetener and salt and blend until you have a crumbly dough.

Line a cupcake tin with baking cases and press the mixture into the bottoms and sides. Bake for about 10 minutes until nice and golden.

Scoop the thick coconut cream from the top of the tin of chilled coconut milk (keep the coconut water for something else) and add it to a large bowl. Add in the cacao powder and sweetener and whisk using an electric mixer.

When the crusts have cooled, remove them from their cases. Fill each one with the filling and sprinkle on some more roasted hazelnuts for decoration.

SLICE AND BAKE CHOCOLATE CHIP COOKIES

GF **DF**

MAKES 12

50 g (2 oz/¼ cup)
coconut oil, softened

75 g (2½ oz/½ cup)
coconut sugar

2 eggs

1 teaspoon vanilla essence

180 g (6 oz/1½ cups)
ground almonds

60 g (2 oz/½ cup)
buckwheat flour

1 teaspoon baking powder

¼ teaspoon salt

60 g (2 oz) dark
chocolate chips

Pictured overleaf

This is a fantastic recipe because you can make one batch of cookie dough and keep it in the freezer for whenever you need a treat. Just slice and bake the amount of cookies you need at the time, so they're always fresh straight from the oven. Perfect chocolate chip cookies are hard to come by but these are close – chewy and oozing with gooey chocolate chips. Serve them warm from the oven with a cold glass of nut milk.

Cream together the soft coconut oil and coconut sugar in a large bowl until you have a smooth mixture. This should take about 1 full minute with an electric mixer.

Whisk in the eggs and vanilla.

In a separate bowl, combine the ground almonds, buckwheat flour, baking powder and salt.

Gradually mix the dry ingredients into the wet, then fold in the chocolate chips.

Divide the cookie dough into two. Use your hands to roll and shape each half into a cylinder shape, then wrap them in cling film. Pop them in the freezer for at least an hour.

Preheat the oven to 180°C/350°F/Gas mark 4.

When the dough is chilled, cut however many cookies you want from the dough. Pop the remaining dough in the freezer.

Lay the cookies out on a baking sheet lined with parchment paper and bake for about 9 minutes. I like to take mine out a little early so they're extra chewy.

'BECAUSE I LOVE YOU' CAKE

GF **DF** **P**

MAKES 1 TWO-TIER CAKE

For the cake:

4 eggs

375 ml (13 fl oz/1½ cups) melted coconut oil, plus extra for greasing

1 teaspoon vanilla essence

375 ml (13 fl oz/1½ cups) maple syrup/honey

480 g (1 lb 10 oz/4 cups) ground almonds

75 g (2½ oz/¾ cup) cacao powder

1 teaspoon coarse salt

2 teaspoons baking powder

For the icing:

2 x 400 ml (13 fl oz) tins coconut milk (kept in the fridge overnight)

60 ml (2 fl oz/¼ cup) maple syrup/honey

1 teaspoon vanilla essence

3 tablespoons cacao powder

TO TOP: strawberries, raspberries and blackberries

This cake is beautifully rich, chocolatey and moist, but not too heavy and the whippy chocolate frosting is just to die for. Pile fresh berries and edible flowers on top and you'll have the most stunning masterpiece, for the eyes and the taste buds! This cake is perfect for birthdays and celebrations, but it also makes the most gorgeous surprise for someone for no occasion at all, simply 'because I love you'.

Preheat the oven to 180°C/350°F/Gas mark 4.

Whisk the eggs, melted coconut oil, vanilla and sweetener together in a large bowl.

In a separate bowl, combine the ground almonds, cacao powder, salt and baking powder.

Gradually add the dry ingredients to the wet.

Line or grease two 20 cm (8 in) cake tins with coconut oil. Divide the mixture evenly and bake for about 35 minutes, until a cake tester comes out clean. While the cakes are baking, take the tins of coconut milk out of the fridge to let them soften.

Let the cakes cool completely, then make the icing.

Scoop the coconut cream from the top of the tins of coconut milk (keep the coconut water for something else). Add it to a large bowl and whisk it together with the sweetener, vanilla and cacao powder until you have a gorgeous whippy frosting. If you're not icing the cake straight away, keep the icing in the fridge until just before.

When the cakes are cool, ice the bottom one, then place the second on top and top with icing. Pile with berries and serve.

PEACH CRUMBLE

GF **DF** **V**

SERVES 4

For the filling:

5 large peaches

4 tablespoons maple syrup/honey

juice of 1 lemon

¼ teaspoon ground nutmeg

½ teaspoon ground cinnamon

For the topping:

100 g (3½ oz/1 cup) gluten-free oats

40 g (1¼ oz/⅓ cup) gluten-free oat flour (see page 11)

25 g (1 oz/¼ cup) flaked almonds

2 tablespoons maple syrup/honey

3 tablespoons melted coconut oil

Crumbles are such an easy, crowd-pleasing classic and here the usual apples or rhubarb are swapped out for some fresh peaches. If you can, make this in high summer when peaches are juicy and ripe and their natural sugar content is at its peak. You can use one 23 cm (9 in) dish or divide the recipe into mini dishes for individual portions.

Preheat the oven to 190°C/375°F/Gas mark 5.

Slice the peaches and add them to a large bowl. Add the sweetener, lemon juice, nutmeg and cinnamon to the bowl and mix well. Pour the peaches and any remaining liquid into your dish and spread them out evenly.

Use the same bowl to make the crumble. Combine the oats, oat flour and flaked almonds. Add in the sweetener and melted coconut oil and mix well.

Sprinkle the crumble generously over the peaches. Cover with foil and bake for 10 minutes, then remove the foil and bake for another 20–25 minutes until the peaches are beautifully soft and the crumble is golden and crisp.

STRAWBERRY TARTS

GF **DF** **V** **P**

MAKES 6

For the crust:

240 g (8½ oz/2 cups) ground almonds

3 tablespoons melted coconut oil

3 tablespoons maple syrup/honey

pinch of coarse salt

For the filling:

300 g (10½ oz/2¼ cups) strawberries

1 tablespoon chia seeds

1 tablespoon maple syrup/honey

1 x 400 ml (13 fl oz) tin coconut milk (kept in the fridge overnight)

Pictured overleaf

These are beyond moreish. The crusts are crumbly and sweet and the scrumptious strawberry filling oozes out of them after the first bite. Each one is topped with a dollop of whipped coconut cream, giving them that classic strawberries and cream flavour. They're perfect individual portions, leaving you satisfied but still wishing you had one more bite!

Preheat the oven to 180°C/350°F/Gas mark 4. Take the tin of coconut milk out of the fridge to allow it to soften a little.

Combine all of the crust ingredients and mix well. You should have a crumbly mixture.

Line a cupcake tin with paper cases and divide the crust mixture among them. I know it looks like it won't stick together, but it will! Use your fingers to press the mixture firmly into the bottoms and up the sides of each paper case. Bake for 9–11 minutes until golden and crisp.

While they're baking, add half of the strawberries to your blender and blend until smooth. Add in the chia seeds and sweetener and blend again. Let the mixture sit for a few minutes to allow the chia seeds to swell and then blend once more. Set it aside to swell even more until you're ready to use it.

When the tart shells are done, take them out and leave to cool.

Fill each one with the strawberry mixture. Slice the remaining strawberries and top each tart with a few slices.

Scoop the coconut cream from the top of the tin of coconut milk (keep the coconut water for something else) and whisk it until smooth and whippy. Top each tart with a dollop of whipped coconut cream before serving.

DRINKS

COCOGO SMOOTHIE

GF DF V P

SERVES 1

½ large mango

175 ml (6 fl oz/¾ cup) cold coconut water

juice of 1 lime

½ teaspoon fresh ginger

¼ teaspoon ground turmeric

This is so creamy and refreshing. The ginger and lime blend with the sweetness of the mango and coconut water for the perfect tropical smoothie. Ginger and turmeric are great for jump-starting your digestive system, so this smoothie is ideal for getting your tummy back on track.

Prepare your mango (remove the skin and stone, etc.) and add it to your blender with all of the other ingredients.

Blend until completely smooth.

DREAMY GREEN SMOOTHIE

SERVES 1

250 ml (8½ fl oz/1 cup) almond milk, unsweetened

½ ripe avocado, pit and skin removed

1 large handful of spinach

2 pitted dates

½ teaspoon vanilla essence

Luxurious and creamy with a velvety smooth hint of vanilla, this is the healthiest milkshake on the planet! The key is to get a perfectly ripe avocado, as that's what makes this so wonderfully creamy. The two dates blend with the vanilla for a gentle sweetness. This smoothie has a lovely blend of healthy fats, iron and fibre, so it makes a great start to the day – or even an afternoon snack when you're in the mood for something that tastes comforting and clean while cleverly keeping those sweet-tooth cravings at bay.

Add everything to your food processor and blend on high until you have a smooth, creamy mixture. Make sure all the dates, avocado and spinach are blended well and there are no chunks.

Pour into your glass and serve cold.

CUCUMBER MINT SLUSHIE

SERVES 1

½ large cucumber

10 g (½ oz) fresh mint

juice of 1 lemon

60 ml (2 fl oz/¼ cup) water

5 ice cubes

OPTIONAL: honey or
maple syrup

This is the best thirst quencher. I had something like this
in a gorgeous health café near Honolulu and then spent ages
trying to recreate it. My version is a little different; it's more
citrusy and doesn't feature any sweetener, but feel free to
add in some honey or maple syrup. I love the crunch of the
crushed ice and it's the most delicious drink on a sunny
day or after a workout.

Juice the cucumber and mint. If you don't have a juicer, blend
them in your food processor and then squeeze through a nut
milk bag into a bowl or jug.

Add the cucumber mint juice to your blender with the lemon
juice, water and ice (add in a little sweetener, too, if you like)
and blend until you have an icy, slushie mixture.

Pour into a glass and serve straight away.

BLUEBERRY BANANA
PROTEIN SHAKE

SERVES 1

250 ml (8½ fl oz/1 cup)
almond milk

½ banana

1 scoop of vanilla protein
powder (I use Sunwarrior)

50 g (2 oz/¼ cup)
blueberries

Sometimes less is more – and this has just a few simple
ingredients. Try it after a workout because it's filling, protein-
packed and tastes like such a treat. For busy mornings, put the
banana, blueberries and protein in a container in the fridge
the night before, then just dump it in your blender with the
almond milk in the morning.

Add everything to your blender and blend until smooth.

Serve cold.

RASPBERRY AND MINT LEMONADE

SERVES 4

juice of 3 lemons

3 tablespoons honey/
maple syrup

750 ml (1⅓ pints/
3½ cups) water

100 g (3½ oz/¾ cup)
raspberries

2 sprigs of fresh mint

ice

This is super refreshing and so delicious, not to mention so pretty, but it's not just for summer – it's a real mood enhancer in the darkness of winter. It's tempting (and still delicious!) to drink it straight away, but leaving the fresh mint to infuse the lemonade before serving makes this extra special.

Add the lemon juice, sweetener and water to your blender and blend to combine.

Add in half of the raspberries and pulse until the mixture turns pink.

Add the mint and the rest of the raspberries to your jug and pour in the pink lemonade.

Pop it in the fridge for about an hour to infuse and then serve over ice.

SWEET TURMERIC AND CINNAMON ALMOND MILK

GF **DF** **V** **P**

**MAKES 1 LITRE
(1³/4 PINTS/4 CUPS)**

300 g (10 oz/
2 cups) almonds

1 litre (1¾ pints/4 cups)
water

1 teaspoon ground turmeric

1 teaspoon ground
cinnamon

2 tablespoons date syrup

This is dreamy. Spiced with turmeric and cinnamon and lightly sweetened with sticky date syrup, this is no ordinary nut milk. It tastes incredible on its own or in a smoothie, and it's absolutely divine heated up as an alternative to tea or coffee. This recipe also works wonders if you use cashews instead of almonds, or a combination of the two.

Soak your almonds the night before. To do this, put the almonds in a large bowl and pour over enough water so that there is about an inch of liquid above them, cover and place them in the fridge.

Drain and rinse the almonds and then add them to your blender with 1 litre of fresh water.

Blitz on high for about a minute until all of the almonds are broken down and you have a cloudy milk.

Add in the turmeric, cinnamon and date syrup and blitz again until combined.

Gradually pour the mixture through your nut milk bag into a jug or bowl, squeezing gently until all of the liquid has passed through.

Store the milk in a bottle or covered jug for up to 3 days. After a day or two, a little separation is normal – just shake before serving.

VANILLA PISTACHIO MILK

GF **DF** **V** **P**

MAKES 1 LITRE (1³/4 PINTS/4 CUPS)

300 g (10 oz/2 cups) pistachios

1 litre (1¾ pints/4 cups) water

1 teaspoon vanilla essence

This nut milk is smooth and beautiful with its gorgeous pale pastel green colour and delicious vanilla aroma. You can add this to porridge, smoothies or simply drink it as it is. Heat it with a little cinnamon and a dribble of maple syrup just before bed and you'll sleep like a baby.

Add the pistachios to a bowl and pour water over them so that they're completely submerged and there's about an inch of liquid above them. Cover and soak in the fridge overnight.

Drain and rinse the pistachios and then add them to your blender with 1 litre of fresh water. Add in the vanilla. Blend on high until you have a smooth, cloudy milk.

Gradually pour the mixture through your nut milk bag into a jug or bowl, squeezing gently until all the liquid has passed through.

Store the milk in a bottle or covered jug in the fridge for up to 3 days. Shake before serving.

ROSEMARY MAPLE TISANE

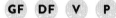

SERVES 2

500 ml (17 fl oz/2 cups) boiling water

1 lemon

2 sprigs of fresh rosemary

2 tablespoons maple syrup

This is inspired by a fantastic rosemary and maple bourbon cocktail that my boyfriend and I love to make. One day, when I wasn't so inclined but still lusting after the gorgeous flavour, I decided to forgo the whisky and heat it up. The result is a soul-warming cup of comfort, so much so that I've picked the little rosemary plant in my kitchen clean.

While your water is coming up to the boil, squeeze the juice from the lemon and add half to each of your serving cups.

Add a sprig of rosemary and a tablespoon of maple syrup to each.

Pour the boiling water in on top and stir well. Let everything infuse for about 5 minutes.

Remove the rosemary and stir once more before serving.

STEAMED ALMOND MILK WITH HONEY AND CINNAMON

GF **DF** **P**

SERVES 1

250 ml (8½ fl oz/1 cup) almond milk

1 teaspoon honey

½ teaspoon ground cinnamon, plus extra for serving

This is one of my favourite things on a chilly evening. It's so simple to prepare and is comforting like nothing else. Frothing it in the blender makes it extra special.

Add the almond milk and honey to a saucepan and place over a medium heat until it is hot.

When it's your desired temperature, add it to your blender with the cinnamon.

Blitz on high until nice and frothy.

Pour into a mug and sprinkle with a little more cinnamon before serving.

RASPBERRY AND ORANGE ICED TEA

**MAKES 1 LITRE
(1³/4 PINTS/4 CUPS)**

2 Earl Grey tea bags

1 litre (1¾ pints/
4 cups) boiling water

1 large orange

100 g (3½ oz/¾ cup)
fresh raspberries

ice

This tastes as good as it looks thanks to Earl Grey's citrus flavour, while the fresh orange and raspberry bring it to a whole new level. Keep a jug in your fridge to sip on throughout the day. It's also great for summer if you feel like having a non-alcoholic tipple that's just as pretty as a cocktail.

Add the tea bags to a large jug and pour over 1 litre of boiling water, to fill up the jug about halfway. Leave to steep for about 15 minutes.

Remove the tea bags and pop the jug in the fridge to chill.

Slice the orange and use a fork to muddle and mash half of the raspberries. Add the orange slices, crushed raspberries and the whole raspberries to the cooled tea. Fill up the jug with ice.

Serve cold with some extra ice.

PANTRY

These are some of my favourite ingredients and the reasons why I use them (and why you should too!). Everything from the bare necessities to some lovely extras to have in your cupboard.

FATS

Coconut oil

Coconut oil has loads of amazing benefits and is absolutely delicious, not to mention versatile. Use it in sweet and savoury cooking and on skin, hair and nails. I even use it on my dog's skin to treat his allergies. So what makes this natural oil so incredible? Although coconut oil is almost 90 per cent saturated fat, not all saturated fats are created equal. Coconut oil is made up of medium-chain fatty acids, which are metabolised by the body in completely different ways than long- or short-chain fatty acids. They're transported directly from the intestines to the liver, where they are more likely to be burned as fuel, as opposed to shorter and longer chains which typically get stored as fat. When used on the skin, they also allow the oil to penetrate the skin deeply, making coconut oil an excellent moisturiser. High vitamin E content and natural ultraviolet protection are added bonuses.

The saturated fats in coconut oil also have antimicrobial properties, which help to combat various bacteria, fungi and parasites that can cause indigestion. About 50 per cent of these fats are lauric acid, which helps to prevent high cholesterol and high blood pressure and supports the immune system and the thyroid. Coconut oil also helps in the absorption of other nutrients such as vitamins, minerals and amino acids.

With its gorgeous subtle smell, taste and bounty of healthy benefits, coconut oil is an amazing ingredient and pops up in loads of these recipes. Because it tolerates high temperatures, it's the perfect substitute for butter and other fats when baking. It gives a unique lightness to cakes, muffins, brownies, etc. while still achieving that same fluffiness and decadence you get when using butter. The coconut aroma is very mild and unobtrusive and shouldn't compromise the other flavours in your dish. Once you've tried coconut oil scrambled eggs you'll never go back!

There are so many brands out there now and many budget options have appeared in supermarkets. While it's great that coconut oil is now widely available, it's also important to find a brand that is virgin and unrefined, as well as meeting your taste requirements. Many of the cheaper brands are very processed, which can diminish the nutrient content of the oil, so it's best to shop around and find a good-quality one.

Olive oil

This Mediterranean staple has the most gorgeous flavour and is velvety smooth, while still tasting fresh and light. It makes a delicious dressing or sauce even just as it is with nothing added. You can also cook with it or use it as the foundation for sauces and dips. Extra virgin olive oil is the most nutrient rich and is full of monounsaturated fats and antioxidants, which help lower blood pressure and cholesterol and reduce inflammation.

Avocados

Like olive oil, avocados are another great source of healthy fats. They're high in monounsaturated fats, which help to reduce blood pressure and cholesterol, and are packed with vitamins B, C and E, which help to fight off disease and infection. They're also high in folate, which is used by the body in cell repair and in the conversion of carbohydrates into energy.

Try avocados with eggs in the mornings, in salads and in smoothies, and they work really well as a thickener in desserts. Another delicious, less common way to enjoy avocados is to cut one in half and remove the stone, then add a teaspoon of honey to its hole and fill with tamari. Grab a spoon and eat it straight out of the skin – one of my mom's favourite snacks!

Coconut milk

Coconut milk is a great alternative to milk or cream. It tastes so luxurious and is perfect for adding a delicious richness to curries, soups and desserts. When coconut milk is mentioned in these recipes, I'm referring to full-fat, tinned coconut milk, not the cartons, which are usually a blend of coconut and rice milk and full of additives. Often the recipes call for coconut milk that has been refrigerated overnight, because this separates the cream from the liquid and leaves you with a layer of coconut cream, which is fabulous in desserts.

NUTS, SEEDS & BEANS

Almonds

Amazing almonds! They are a great source of vitamin E, calcium, magnesium and potassium, are rich in protein and fibre and naturally low in sugar. They are also high in monounsaturated fats, which have been known to reduce cholesterol and lower the risk of heart disease, as well as being extremely alkaline, which is great for your immune system. Try using almond flour as a flour substitute as it has a gorgeous flavour and texture and is much more nutritious than white flour. In the recipes it is listed as ground almonds, as many people find almond flour hard to find. The two are almost identical, the only difference being that the almonds in almond flour are more finely ground.

Almond milk

Almond milk is a great dairy-free alternative to cow's milk. It's great for vegans and anyone limiting their dairy intake. It contains no cholesterol and is naturally low in calories and fat. Compared to other dairy-free alternatives, like soy and rice milk, almond milk has the highest concentrations of vitamins and minerals, containing calcium, zinc, iron and magnesium, to name a few.

Although now widely available in many flavours and in both unsweetened and sweetened versions, when buying it in the shop it's best to stick to the unsweetened and unflavoured kind to avoid any refined sugars or artificial flavours that often sneak into the commercial versions. When you can, it's always best to make your own. It tastes much creamier, much fresher and it doesn't contain any stabilisers or gums. See page 12 to see how to make it.

Cashews

Cashews have an incredible flavour and you can use them in loads of clever ways as a substitute for flour, cream and even cheese! Compared to other nuts, they have a low fat content and they're cholesterol free. They're also high in calcium and magnesium and full of proanthocyanidins, which fight against cancer tumour cells by preventing them from dividing any further. Pretty amazing for a little nut.

Chia seeds

Chia seeds are full of nutrients and will give you a lot of nutritional bang for your buck. They're gluten free, packed with protein and high in fibre and antioxidants, making them great for your digestive and immune systems. They are also a great source of omega 3 fatty acids. Chia seeds can be used in so many ways – simply sprinkle on whatever you're eating or add to baked goods. Alternatively, make the most of their gelatinous abilities in chia pudding (page 28) or as a vegan substitute for eggs.

CHIA SEED EGG SUBSTITUTE RECIPE
To replace 1 egg

1 tablespoon ground chia seeds

3 tablespoons water

If you can't find ground chia seeds in the shop, simply add them to a high-powered food processor and blitz until fine.

Combine the water and ground chia seeds in a bowl and mix well. Let it sit for a few minutes until thick. Mix again and let it sit for another few minutes until the mixture is a similar texture to a raw egg.

Sunflower and pumpkin seeds

Sunflower and pumpkin seeds are another great source of healthy fats, vitamins and minerals. Sunflower seeds are high in folate and vitamin E, while pumpkin seeds are rich in iron and zinc. These little seeds are easy to sneak into your diet – you can sprinkle toasted seeds on almost everything from salads and soups to porridge and desserts. To learn how to toast them, see page 13.

Pecans

Pecans are rich in monounsaturated fats, antioxidants and vitamin E and are so flavourful. They taste even better toasted and are incredible in sweet and savoury dishes.

Pistachios

Pistachios have the most beautiful colour and their flavour is like nothing else. Sweet or savoury, you can sprinkle them on anything for a pop of colour as well as taste. Like almonds and cashews, they're a good source of protein and fats and rich in vitamin E.

Tahini

Tahini is sesame seed paste and has a powerful, rich flavour. It's commonly used to make hummus, but also tastes divine in dressings, sauces and even desserts. Try using light tahini, rather than dark, as the flavour is a little milder and it's lovely and smooth.

Chickpeas

You can use chickpeas, or garbanzo beans, in salads, curries, falafels and home-made hummus. They're high in protein, full of dietary fibre – so they're great for digestive health – and they contain iron, calcium, phosphate, magnesium, zinc and vitamin K, which help to keep our bones strong. They also contain lots of folate to keep your heart healthy and help reduce high blood pressure. You can either use dried chickpeas and soak them overnight, or tinned chickpeas, which are already soaked. You can just grab a tin from the back of the cupboard at the last minute; it's so great if you haven't planned ahead. However, some tinned chickpeas contain lots of added salt, so make sure to read the label and find one with little to no added sodium.

Chickpea flour, also called gram flour, is made from ground, dried chickpeas. It has an amazing texture and can be used in sweet and savoury dishes in so many wonderful ways. Use it in breads (page 112), fritters (page 38) and a host of other dishes.

GRAINS

Grains have become somewhat taboo for some people, but it's all about picking the right ones. Quinoa and buckwheat are so delicious and there are endless creative ways to experiment with them.

Quinoa

Quinoa is one of the original superfoods and is an incredible wheat-free alternative to other grains. Although cooked like a grain, quinoa is actually a seed, which if not harvested, sprouts into a vegetable like spinach or chard. Quinoa is an amazing source of protein. It's one of the most protein-packed foods we can eat, containing all nine essential amino acids – very handy for vegetarians or anyone avoiding meat. It's also extremely high in fibre, containing almost twice as much as regular grains, and gluten free, making it great for coeliacs or anyone staying away from gluten. To cap it all off, it has a low glycaemic index and contains loads of antioxidants and minerals such as magnesium, iron and zinc.

When cooked correctly, quinoa is gorgeous and fluffy, with a slight nutty aroma that absorbs sauces and flavours incredibly. Head to page 10 to see the foolproof recipe for perfect quinoa.

Buckwheat

Despite its name, buckwheat isn't a form of wheat. It's actually related to rhubarb and is naturally gluten free. Buckwheat is rich in flavonoids, which help protect against disease, are great for heart health and controlling blood sugar and high in fibre. Use buckwheat 'groats', which are funky-looking triangular kernels, in a similar way to quinoa. Also, do try buckwheat flour, which is fantastic for baking – think gorgeous fluffy pancakes and beautiful crumbly scones. With a Japanese grandmother, I grew up with lots of Japanese food to hand. Our fridge was always stocked with cold buckwheat noodles, or soba, ready for snacks. Nowadays, I use them a little more sparingly, instead of regular pasta or in Pho (page 99). You can pick them up in any health shop, Asian market and in lots of supermarkets.

Gluten-free oats

Oats are one of the most classic breakfast ingredients and gluten-free oats are now available in most supermarkets. Oats are full of fibre and are filling and satisfying, making them a great option for breakfast. Use them in overnight oats, bircher muesli and in crumbles and granolas. You can also grind oats in your food processor to make your own oat flour for baking (page 11).

SWEETENERS

The sweeteners here are all natural sugars, making them the lesser of two evils, but they should still be eaten in moderation as part of a balanced diet.

Dates

Dates are jam-packed with essential nutrients, minerals and vitamins such as vitamin A, iron, potassium and calcium. They're also high in fibre, making them great for digestive health, and rich in magnesium, which helps to reduce blood pressure and acts as a natural anti-inflammatory.

Use them in the recipes as a natural sweetener, adding a gorgeous chewiness to baked goods. If you can, opt for Medjool dates as they're particularly sweet with an extra-soft texture.

Coconut sugar

Coconut sugar is loaded with vitamin C and amino acids and is a great substitute for white sugar. Despite it's name, it barely tastes like coconut at all and has a subtle caramel taste.

Maple syrup

Maple syrup is my favourite liquid sweetener. It has the most incredible flavour and is the perfect sweetness. Pure maple syrup contains vitamins, minerals and antioxidants, making it much more nutritious than table sugar. When buying maple syrup, make sure to look for it in a pure form as many store-bought options are just maple-flavoured syrup, full of additives and artificial sweeteners. You want the real, viscous, grade-A liquid amber.

Raw honey

Honey is another natural sweet alternative to sugar. Honey is full of vitamins, minerals and antioxidants and has a beautiful natural flavour. Raw honey is totally unheated, unpasteurized and unprocessed and is an even better alternative to store-bought honeys. If you can, it's best to buy local honey, so keep an eye out at farmers' markets.

TASTE BOOSTERS

Herbs and spices

Even the simplest dish becomes special when you add fresh, pungent herbs and/or a spicy kick. All fresh herbs are great, but basil, coriander, sage, rosemary and mint all taste amazing with pretty much anything. As for spices, you can never have too many! The ones that make a great starter pack if you're filling a pantry are cinnamon, turmeric, paprika, cumin, ginger, cayenne, garam masala, garlic powder and onion powder.

Fresh garlic is added to many of the savoury dishes in this book. As well as tasting amazing, it also has loads of nutritional benefits. Garlic is a rich source of vitamin C, vitamin B16 and manganese, is great for boosting your immune system and can help lower blood pressure and cholesterol. Mince it, roast it, even pickle it for impact.

Vinegar

Vinegars are, of course, amazing in dressings and sauces and some, such as apple cider vinegar, have great nutritional benefits, too. Apple cider vinegar is great for your digestive system and blood pressure. A rich, dark balsamic vinegar is another delicious pantry staple.

Tamari

Tamari is a wonderful Japanese ingredient that features in lots of the recipes and is a definite pantry essential for me. Very similar to soy sauce (both are made from fermented soya beans, but tamari is less salty, a little thicker and doesn't contain any gluten), use it in dressings, sauces and as a seasoning or dip on its own.

Coarse salt

Lots of these recipes, sweet and savoury, use a coarse sea salt. Sea salt is generally much less processed than regular table salt and it also has a much nicer flavour. Although all salt should be used in moderation, it is a necessary flavouring for many dishes and the large flakes in sea salt make it easier to control portions. Try adding a little coarse salt to home-made dark chocolate. It makes the chocolate seem a little sweeter, meaning that you can decrease the amount of natural sugars in your chocolate. Good choices are Maldon sea salt and French fleur de sel.

Cacao powder

Many people are confused by the difference between cacao and cocoa. Cacao powder comes from the cacao bean and is raw, unprocessed and extremely rich in nutrients. Cocoa, on the other hand, comes from cleaned, roasted and processed beans. Raw cacao is full of antioxidants and an excellent source of essential fatty acids, fibre, iron, copper, zinc, magnesium, calcium and sulphur. However, cocoa, as it has been roasted and processed, loses much of these nutritional benefits.

In these recipes I always use cacao powder as opposed to cocoa powder and I have come to love its taste and extra richness. Cacao is one of Nature's greatest superfoods, containing the highest concentration of antioxidants of any known food, more so than blueberries, green tea and even goji berries!

Dark chocolate

Dark chocolate is a great way to treat yourself without overindulging and if you pick a quality, high-percentage dark chocolate it can be quite nutritious. Dark chocolate with a high cocoa content contains antioxidants, fibre and minerals such as iron, magnesium and zinc. Make sure to opt for a brand that is at least 75 per cent cocoa, has a low sugar content and as few additives as possible. If you are vegan or are following a paleo diet make sure to use a dairy-free chocolate in all of these recipes.

TOOL KIT

Everything there is to know about kitchen equipment – from everyday essentials to luxuries for the hard-core healthie.

Cup measures
On my blog I use cup measurements in all my recipes. I know a lot of people aren't used to them, so for this book I have converted everything into grams, too. Cups are a measure of volume rather than weight, which means that once you're used to them, you'll be able to visualize amounts, making it easier for you to experiment with your own recipes or tweak things to your liking. The cup measures I use are standard cup measures, not a mug or tea cup. If you don't have cup measures but would like to start using them, you can get them in any kitchen shop and in many supermarkets.

Spoon measures
I use actual spoon measures when referring to teaspoons and tablespoons in my recipes. Cutlery sizes can really vary, so investing in a proper set is wise. You'd be surprised how much ¼ or ½ teaspoon really is when you use spoon measures!

Spiralizer
Spiralizers are a revelation. Who knew changing the shape and texture of vegetables could make such a difference to how they taste. You can't beat a bowl of courgetti smothered in bolognese sauce or some crispy, curly sweet potato fries hot out of the oven. There are lots of different kinds of spiralizers and although the different types have their benefits, a little hand-held one is very useful. It's really simple to use and clean and so easy to store, which is especially important if you have a small kitchen, like I do, where space is at a premium.

Food processor/blender
A food processor or blender is required for lots of these recipes. They're great for making soups, sauces and smoothies and for grinding nuts or making nut butters. I use a Vitamix, which is extremely powerful and has a price tag to match. I've also used a Nutribullet and Kenwood Multipro food processor, which work well too, so buy the best you can afford.

Garlic mincer

A garlic mincer will make your life so much easier – you don't even have to peel the cloves! I rely on a really simple one from Ikea. There is fresh garlic in loads of these recipes and no one wants to be stuck with the job of mincing garlic, so one of these is the perfect little hack. You'll save loads of time and get perfectly minced garlic.

Nut milk bag

This is the only thing standing between you and gorgeous home-made nut milk. It is nothing more than a simple filtering tool, is reusable and can be found online and in good health shops. I use mine all the time to make all kinds of fresh home-made nut milks.

Mandolin

A mandolin grater is by no means a necessity, but using one adds something special to a dish. They grate things into really thin slices so they're perfect for making vegetable crisps or for adding raw vegetables to salads that will really catch a dressing's flavour. Mind you, don't slice yourself in the process.

Chargrill pan

Living in a place like Ireland, with less than ideal weather and lots of rain, means barbecuing is a rare treat and sometimes you just need that smoky taste and those scrummy char lines. A chargrill pan is a great way to get the look and taste from the comfort of your own kitchen. Use for everything from burgers and chicken to fresh fruit and vegetables.

STOCKISTS

Select Stores

Dalkey, Co. Dublin

I grew up in beautiful Dalkey village and lived there all my life until the age of 21. Not only is it my home, but it's also home to the best health shop in the country. No matter what you're looking for, Oliver and the team at Select Stores have it. They serve amazing smoothies and juices and the yummiest healthy breakfast around.

Nourish

Multiple Dublin locations

All of the Nourish stores have great stock and just about everything you could possibly need. Their online shopping is a saviour. You can have everything delivered anywhere in Ireland or the UK in a few days, which is great if you're short on time and need to stock up.

Asian markets

Asian markets are great for stocking up on budget nuts, dates and coconut products as well as all the amazing Asian ingredients you can't get anywhere else. In Dublin, I go to the Asian Market on Drury Street for sushi vinegar, nori, wasabi, soba noodles and miso paste, as well as their fresh vegetables, herbs and so much more. It's fun to shop somewhere different and the products are authentic and usually much cheaper.

Fallon & Byrne

Exchequer Street, Dublin 2

Fallon & Byrne is a treasure trove of beautiful and hard-to-find ingredients. It's a lot more expensive than regular supermarkets, so I reserve shopping there for treats and emergencies (often it's the only place to get certain things), but I would happily roam the aisles for hours. They have the most gorgeous seasonal fruit and vegetables – just looking at them fills me with recipe inspiration – and a great butcher and fishmonger for whenever I can afford to splurge on the good stuff.

Avoca

Multiple locations around Ireland

Avoca is one of my favourite stores and there are particularly good branches in Kilmacanogue and Monkstown. They have the fabulous James Whelan butchers, great fruit and vegetables and have recently upped their game even more, stocking loads of wonderful health food ingredients. Plus, they sell some lovely homeware, so it's a joy to mosey around the shop while you decide what to make for dinner.

The Organic Supermarket
Blackrock, Rathgar and Malahide
(all Dublin)
The Organic Supermarket's online shop is
another Irish site that I use if I'm organized
enough to know what I need in advance.
They also have shops around Dublin.
They carry most health food products and
lovely organic fruit and veg. They offer
same day delivery in Dublin, too, which
has saved me more than once during a few
kitchen disasters.

The Health Store
Multiple locations mostly around Dublin
The Health Store shops are usually cleverly
located next to big supermarkets, which
is ideal for adding harder-to-find extras to
your weekly shop. From almond butter
to Epsom salts, they've got it.

Evergreen Healthfoods
Multiple locations around Galway
If you live in Galway, you're probably lucky
enough to have one of these close by. They
have seven shops and a great online store,
so those of us further away don't have to
miss out.

Whole Foods Market
UK and US
Whole Foods is a one-stop shop for
everything you could possibly need.
From quinoa pasta to natural beauty
products and everything in between.
Whenever I travel to the US, I scour the
shelves and smuggle back new products
that haven't made it across the pond yet.
My only gripe is that we don't have one
back home.

Planet Organic
Multiple London locations
Planet Organic is another fabulous
supermarket for all things healthy. As
they are more expensive than regular
supermarkets, shopping here is a treat
rather than a weekly occurrence, but
you'll certainly enjoy it when you do.
They're scattered around London and
you can shop online, too.

Amazon
As we all know, Amazon has everything!
I use it to buy most of my kitchen gadgets
and utensils, but it's also quite handy
for those hard-to-find ingredients
(ahem, quinoa flour) and things like
nut milk bags.

INDEX

ACKNOWLEDGEMENTS

I'd like to thank the amazing team at Ebury –
Lizzy Gray for taking a chance on me and Louise
McKeever for all of her hard work to make this
beautiful book what it is. Thank you to Smith &
Gilmour for their wonderful design work and a huge
thank you to my food shoot team for bringing my
recipes to life, more beautifully than I could have
ever imagined: Martin Poole for his incredibly
gorgeous photography, Aya Nishimura for her
stunning food styling and Charlotte O'Connell for
helping to recreate all of my recipes so perfectly.